T0329298

Cambridge Elements ≡

Elements in Religion and Violence
edited by
James R. Lewis
University of Tromsø
and
Margo Kitts
Hawai'i Pacific University

OPEN SOURCE JIHAD

*Problematizing the Academic Discourse on Islamic
Terrorism in Contemporary Europe*

Per-Erik Nilsson
Uppsala University, Sweden

CAMBRIDGE
UNIVERSITY PRESS

CAMBRIDGE
UNIVERSITY PRESS

University Printing House, Cambridge CB2 8BS, United Kingdom

One Liberty Plaza, 20th Floor, New York, NY 10006, USA

477 Williamstown Road, Port Melbourne, VIC 3207, Australia

314–321, 3rd Floor, Plot 3, Splendor Forum, Jasola District Centre,
New Delhi – 110025, India

79 Anson Road, #06–04/06, Singapore 079906

Cambridge University Press is part of the University of Cambridge.

It furthers the University's mission by disseminating knowledge in the pursuit of
education, learning, and research at the highest international levels of excellence.

www.cambridge.org
Information on this title: www.cambridge.org/9781108448741
DOI: 10.1017/9781108552233

First published 2018

A catalogue record for this publication is available from the British Library.

ISBN 978-1-108-44874-1 Paperback
ISSN 2397-9496 (online)
ISSN 2514-3786 (print)

Cambridge Elements

Open Source Jihad

Problematizing the Academic Discourse on Islamic Terrorism in Contemporary Europe

Per-Erik Nilsson

*Financed by The Swedish Research Council
(ref. nr. 2016-01944)*

ABSTRACT: In *Open Source Jihad*, Per-Erik Nilsson provides a unique overview of the academic research and political legislation concerning "Islamic terrorism" in Europe. He scrutinizes in detail how the concepts "terrorism," "radicalization," and "counterterrorism" have developed as academic objects of study and political objects of governance. In the Element, Nilsson brings to the fore systemic problems of the field of terrorism studies as well as the various anti-terrorist apparatuses developed by EU member states. *Open Source Jihad* should be required reading for anyone interested in current European political and social events.

KEYWORDS: Europe, terrorism, radizalization, discourse, counterterrorism

© Per-Erik Nilsson 2018
ISBNs: 9781108448741 (PB) 9781108552233 (OC)
DOI: 10.1017/9781108552233

Contents

Open Source Jihad

Looking back at the beginnings of academic research on terrorism just over 40 years ago, it is extraordinary to see that what was once a marginal subject for social science has developed into a full-fledged program of "terrorism studies."
– Martha Crenshaw

The message as a whole then becomes paradoxical and the paradoxes and contradictions manifest in different ways: exceptional circumstances yet normal; outside society yet within; the threat from small groups yet measures for everyone.
– Andrés Perezalon

The Looming Specter of 9/11

Open Source Jihad, the main title of this Element, is taken from a recurring section in Al-Qaida on the Arabic Peninsula's (AQAP) magazine *Inspire*. The section is informative and describes various forms of techniques that might come in handy for the "jihadist" planning an attack in the West. The instructions range from disassembling and cleaning an AK47, shooting stances with your newly cleaned weapon, smuggling a bomb onto an airplane, and stalking high-value targets. *Open Source Jihad* is also a suitable name for the relatively recent academic field of terrorism studies and especially so the subfield focusing on "Islamic terrorism." Terrorism studies emerged in the 1970s but virtually exploded after 9/11.[1] Since then, the publication of academic peer-reviewed articles rose by 300 percent the following year; some estimations show that a new book is being published every sixth hour.[2] The thirst for knowledge about

[1] See Andrew Silke, "The Devil You Know: Continuing problems with research on terrorism," *Terrorism and Political Violence* 13(4) (2001), 1–14.

[2] Magnus Ranstorp, "Mapping Terrorism Studies After 9/11: An academic field of old problems and new prospects," in *Critical Terrorism Studies: A new research agenda*, eds.

terrorism still seems never ending. Today terrorism studies have developed into a vast academic field with several renowned academic journals (e.g., *Terrorism and Political Violence*, *Studies in Conflict & Terrorism*, and *Critical Studies on Terrorism*), comprehensive encyclopedias of terrorism,[3] founding authors,[4] and academic experts frequently appearing in the news media.[5]

However, the study of terrorism has been and still is suffering from a number of shortcomings, not least since terrorism has been treated like an open source for speculation, moralizing, and career opportunities.[6] Michel Stohl even argues that the field is maintained "on a diet of fast food research: quick, cheap, ready-to-hand and nutritionally dubious."[7] One example is the former terrorism expert Alexis Debat, who managed to rise to the high ranks in the world of US think tanks and news media through a made-up CV and an impressive bundle of lies.[8] Regarding the academic

Richard Jackson, Marie Breen Smyth, and Jeroem Gunning (London and New York: Routledge, 2009), 17.

[3] Peter Chalk, *Encyclopedia of Terrorism* (Oxford: ABC-Clio, 2012); James Ciment, ed., *World Terrorism: An encyclopedia of political violence from ancient times to the post-9/11 era* (London and New York: Routledge, 2011); Martha Crenshaw and John Pimlott, eds., *International Encyclopedia of Terrorism* (London and New York: Routledge, 1998); Harvey W. Kushner, ed., *Encyclopedia of Terrorism* (London: Sage Publications, 2003); Gus Martin, ed., *The SAGE Encyclopedia of Terrorism* (London: Sage Publications, 2011).

[4] E.g., Martha Crenshaw, Walter Laqeur, and Robert Pape.

[5] In Europe, e.g., Gilles Kepel, Magnus Ranstorp, and Olivier Roy.

[6] See Lisa Stampnitzky, *Disciplining Terror. How Experts Invented "Terrorism"* (Cambridge: Cambridge University Press, 2013).

[7] Michael Stohl, "Don't Confuse Me with the Facts: Knowledge claims and terrorism,," *Critical Studies on Terrorism* 5(1) (2012), 32 [31–49].

[8] Guillemette Faure and Pascal Riché, "Comment Alexis Debat a trompé tout Washington," *Rue* 89, September 14, 2010, accessed February 15, 2015, http://rue89.nouvelobs.com/2007/09/14/comment-alexis-debat-a-trompe-tout-washington-2873.

study of terrorism, Richard Jackson argues that the orthodox or mainstream school of terrorism (MTS) is suffering from bias in terms of using poor methods and theories, being state-centric, being uncritical, and having compromisingly close ties to state interests.[9] As such, terrorism has developed into an objective backdrop for understanding and interpreting contemporary violent acts directed against nation-states while state violence is usually excluded.[10] Although the whole field of mainstream terrorism studies should not be reduced to these points, examples of publications bearing these traits are not hard to find. One example is the Swedish report *Hot mot demokrati och värdegrund – en lägesbild från Malmö* (A Threat Against Democracy – The Case of Malmö) published in 2009.

Knowledge without Sources

The report was ordered by the then-liberal-conservative Swedish government that called upon the Center for Assymetric Threat and Terrorism Studies (CATS) at the Swedish National Defense College to produce a research overview of the state of affairs regarding "extremism prone to violence [våldsbejakande extremism] and radicalisation."[11] The report turned out to be a case study of the neighborhood of Rosengård in Malmö, Sweden's third-largest city. Rosengård in public debate is almost exclusively associated with

[9] Richard Jackson, "The Core Commitments of Critical Terrorism Studies," *European Political Science* 6(3) (2007), 244–251. See also Arun Kundnani, *The Muslims Are Coming* (London: Verso, 2014), 21.

[10] See Richard Jackson, Marie Breen Smyth, and Jeroen Gunning, eds., *Critical Terrorism Studies: A new research agenda* (London and New York: Routledge, 2009).

[11] Magnus Ranstorp and Josefine Dos Santos, *Hot mot demokrati och värdegrund – en lägesbild från Malmö* (Stockholm: Försvarshögskolan, 2009a), accessed February 15, 2016, www.mah.se/upload/Forskningscentrum/MIM/2009%20Sem inars/vardegrund_175076a.pdf.

such negative categories as violence, car burnings, Islamization, and racism against whites: an image that is uncritically reproduced in the report. In an article summarizing the report, the authors state that out of 22,000 inhabitants, 60 percent of the population were born outside Sweden and another 26 percent have parents born outside Sweden. According to the authors, this large population of first- and so-called second-generation immigrants suffer "extreme segregation" that leads to "an evil spiral" of "bitterness and contempt" resulting in isolation from Swedish society. While the authors appear to embark on a discussion of discrimination and the high thresholds for fully entering into the Swedish society, the authors stress that the main problem of the population in Rosengård is a lack of comprehension of basic values, democracy, and equality. This is seen, not least, in how "ultra-radical Islamists" who preach an extremist Islamist agenda based on hate against the West have created a veritable *Hisbah* – religious police forcing women to veil, separating young boys and girls, and ultimately enforcing patriarchal structures of power.[12] A dire situation indeed.

The picture painted of Rosengård could just as well be that of any other stigmatized borough, suburb, or big city neighborhood such as Clichy-sous-Bois in Paris, Molenbeek in Brussels, or Tower Hamlets in London. These are the infamous "no-go zones" for the average non-Muslim, white citizen.[13] At least this is what was suggested on Fox News by the American security analyst

---

[12] Magnus Ranstorp and Josefine Dos Santos, "Kommuner måste hejda extremism," Svenska Dadbladet, January 28, 2009, accessed January 11, 2016, www.svd.se/kommuner-maste-hejda-extremism.

[13] Carol Matlack, "Debunking the Myth of Muslim-Only Zones in Major European Cities: Stories about big Western cities surrendering neighborhoods to control of Islamist extremists are shocking—and totally false," *Bloomberg Business*, January 14, 2015, accessed February 12, 2016, www.bloomberg.com/news/articles/2015-01-14/debunking-the-muslim-nogo-zone-myth.

Nolan Peterson, who, in the wake of the attacks in Paris in January 2015, declared that areas in central Paris reminded him of a Baghdad where Sharia law reigns.[14] That these areas are also frequented by the average white beer-drinking and ham-eating hipster seemed to have slipped through the observational lens of Peterson. Fox News and Peterson have been mocked by French news media for mistaking these zones for what are called Sensible Urban Zones (*Zones urbaines sensible*),[15] a designation that has to do more with class than anything else. However, there is an irony here. In France, the very idea of no-go zones is in itself not shocking; it is reproduced on a daily basis by politicians in French news media where it is most commonly associated with the metropolitan suburbs,[16] as if Peterson was criticized more for getting the Parisian map wrong than the idea of the no-go zone itself.

Nonetheless, in the Swedish Report the authors set out to understand the degree of radicalization in Rosengård. The analysis draws its empirical material from thirty interviews conducted with state and municipal functionaries, mainly from the police, schools, and social services. As the authors state, their interest is primarily Islamic radicalization, which is noteworthy since this is treated as a commonsensical truism in need of no explanation. No field work in Rosengård

[14] Fox News, "French 'no-go zones' in question after Paris terror attacks," January 9, 2015, accessed February 15, 2015, http://video.foxnews.com/v/3980744730001/french-no-go-zones-in-question-after-paris-terror-attacks/?#sp=show-clips.

[15] E.g., Canal +. "*Le petit journal*,," January 14, 2015, accessed February 15, 2016, www.canalplus.fr/c-emissions/c-le-petit-journal/pid6515-le-petit-journal.html?vid=1197745.

[16] Mustafa Dikeç, "Voices into Noises: Ideological determination of unarticulated justice movements," *Space and Polity* 8(2) (2004), 191–208; Didier Fassin, *Enforcing Order: An ethnography of urban policing* (Cambridge: Polity Press, 2013); Michel Kokoreff, *Sociologie des émeutes* (Paris: Payot, 2008); Laurent Mucchielli, *L'invention de la violence: Des peurs, des chiffres, des faites* (Paris: Fayard, 2011).

and no interviews with ultra-radical Islamists or with the Muslim youth these radicals were supposedly radicalizing are accounted for. Radicalization is taken as a fact, implicitly equivalent to Islamization, immigration, extremism, and violence. This is evident not least in the highly normative and leading formulations of the questions posed to the interview subjects.[17] For example, the question "What are the motives leading to radicalization (hate against society/the West, the war in Iraq, negative personal experiences, etc.)?" not only assumes that radicalization exists, it also proposes answers to why it exists.

The authors present a number of criteria that might be a sign of radicalization. Considering that teenagers are the supposed main targets of radicalization, some of these criteria are indeed curious, for example, frequent mosque visits, growing a beard, watching foreign-TV broadcasts with violent content, practicing physically demanding sports, or lacking a father figure.[18] Were it not for the criteria of travel to war zones and known jihadi training sites, the criteria could potentially be applicable to any devout or occasionally practicing Muslim teenager in Sweden. Moreover, nowhere do the authors state that these criteria have actually resulted in radicalization (i.e., "that a person supports or commits acts of terrorism").[19] They simply state that they might, as if the individuals concerned are potentially and perpetually predisposed to radicalization. In fact, the predetermining and proscriptive factors in the report are Islam and the Middle East, where Islamic violence is treated as quintessentially different from other forms of violence, be it Christian, Buddhist, nationalist, or secular. In other words, without the Islamic factor, the criterion of radicalization is just a description of what could just as easily be described as "rebellious" or "alternative" teenagers.

---

[17] Ranstorp and Dos Santos, "Kommuner måste hejda extremism," 8.

[18] Ranstorp and Dos Santos, "Kommuner måste hejda extremism," 10–11.

[19] Ranstorp and Dos Santos, "Kommuner måste hejda extremism," 3.

Now, as will become clear in this Element, the conclusions drawn by authors of the Rosengård Report fit very well into mainstream explicatory models of terrorism where the religion (Islam), culture (medieval), and social alienation (chosen) are taken as root causes for radicalization.[20] The problem I want to highlight here, however, is less about the assumptions made about Islamic radicalization within mainstream terrorism studies than that these assumptions are given as evidence without any empirical evidence.

I am not the first to highlight these aspects of the Rosengård Report. After its publication, it was widely criticized by leading scholars on Islam in Sweden for being empirically vague and ethnocentric. When these critical voices demanded access to the empirical material, it transpired that it had, in supposedly good academic tradition, been destroyed.[21] Moreover, the head of the Swedish Security Service (*Säkerhetspolisen*) responded by stating that the threat against Sweden and Swedish interests at the time was "very low" and that the negative image of Rosengård is simply wrong: "It's probably due to a misrepresentation by the news media. Rosengård works really well."[22] Even though the report's academic, empirical, and methodological quality has been questioned by nonnegligible parts of the Swedish research community, the report is still treated as the truth. When one of the authors rebutted the critique, he stated that the important thing was to

---

20 See Mark Sedgwick, "The Concept of Radicalization as a Source of Confusion," *Terrorism and Political Violence* 22(4) (2010), 479–494; Floris Vermeulen, "Suspect Communities – Targeting Violent Extremism at the Local Level: Policies of engagement in Amsterdam, Berlin, and London," *Terrorism and Political Violence*, 26(2) (2014), 286–306.

21 TT, "Källmaterialet är förstört," Svenska dagbladet, January 30, 2009, accessed January 15, 2016, https://www.svd.se/kallmaterial-ar-forstort.

22 Kenan Habul, "Säpochefen sågar Rosengårdsrapport," *Sydsvenskan*, June 13, 2009, accessed January 15, 2016, www.sydsvenskan.se/sverige/sapochefen-sagar-rosen gardsrapport/.

not let any potential shortcomings in quality lead to a loss of focus on the matter, namely radicalization in Rosengård.[23]

The Discourse on Islamic Terrorism

The Rosengård Report is but one example of the many ways in which what will henceforth be referred to the as the "discourse on Islamic terrorism" has been reproduced. It is a discourse that, as noted by Peter Jackson, is made out of specific types of categories: "'the Islamic world', 'the West', 'the Islamic revival', 'political Islam', 'Islamism', 'extremism', 'radicalism', 'fundamentalism', 'religious terrorism', 'jihadists', 'Wahhabis', 'Salafis', 'militants', 'moderates', 'global jihadist movement', 'al-Qaeda', and finally, 'Islamic terrorism.'"[24] These categories are, as Jackson notes, "often vaguely defined (if at all), yet culturally loaded and highly flexible in the way they are deployed."[25]

The discourse has now, through its omnipresence in the news media, popular culture, and political speech, become so normalized that it has developed into a language that is on virtually everybody's tongue.[26] As Joseba Zulaika points out, the central mantra of this language is the following: "It is not *if*, but *when*."[27] This is what makes these attacks resonate so widely throughout Western Europe, and be experienced as happenings next door in

---

[23] Magnus Ranstorp, "Diskutera sakfrågan om Rosengård istället," *Svenska Dagbladet*, February 14, 2009, accessed January 12, 2016, www.svd.se/diskutera-sakfragan-om-rosengard-istallet.

[24] Peter Jackson, "Constructing Enemies: 'Islamic terrorism' in academic and political discourse," *Government and Opposition* 42(3) (2007), 401.

[25] Jackson, "Constructing,," 7.

[26] Joshua Woods, "Framing Terror: An experimental framing effects study of the perceived threat of terrorism," *Critical Studies on Terrorism* 4(2) (2011), 199–217.

[27] Joseba Zulaika, *Terrorism: The Self-Fulfilling Prophecy* (Chicago: University of Chicago Press), 158.

a small city such as Norrtälje, north of Stockholm, or in a country such as Latvia, with an estimated population of about 2,000 Muslims. It is moreover structured on binary pairs that draw on Orientalism, Eurocentrism, Imperialism, and state centrism – that is, good/evil, Christianity/Islam, secularism/religion, civilization/barbarity, democracy/terrorism, masculine/feminine, peace/war, just war/unjust war, deradicalization/radicalization, the West/the Orient, and we/them.[28]

These categories, moreover, are part of articulating different types of subjects that are tied to temporality, spatiality, and ontology and displace these subjects from the here and now[29]: temporality in terms of the pre-modernity associated with these subjects but also in terms of their potential for future action,[30] spatially in the locating of them either in the imagined Orient and its border areas within the European nation-state – the suburb. As for the ontology of who "we" the Europeans are and who "they" the radicalized or potentially radicalized Muslims are, as the report so painstakingly testifies, there is, in this logic, no need to talk with "them," since we already know who "they" *really* are.[31] This is a foreclosed logic where the Muslim youth *tout court* is seen as prone to radicalization.[32] A suspected community of Muslim youth is created and portrayed to be in perpetual need of surveillance and discipline for "our"

---

[28] See Arshin Adib-Moghaddam, *A Metahistory of the Clash of Civilizations: Us and them beyond Orientalism* (London: Hurst, 2011); Helen Dexter, "Terrorism and Violence: Another violence is possible?" *Critical Studies on Terrorism* 5(1) (2012), 121–137.

[29] See Jane Samson, *Race and Empire* (New York: Pearson Longman, 2005).

[30] Zulaika, Terrorism.

[31] Per-Erik Nilsson, "Who Is Madame M? Staking Out the Borders for Secular France," in *Religion as a Category of Governance and Sovereignty*, eds. Trevor Stack, Timothy Fitzgerald, and Naomi Goldenberg (Leiden: Brill, 2015), 21–37.

[32] Kundnani, "The Muslims Are Coming."

well-being.[33] This logic calls for and legitimizes a preemptive logic of deradicalization explicitly targeting young Muslims. For this community not to be classified as prone to radicalization and violent extremism, it has to abandon its Islamic identity altogether, as all "not-in-my-name" campaigns bear witness to.[34] The uncanny paradox here is that it is only as Muslims that they can distance themselves from Islam. The community is doomed to eternal stigmatization or mimicry.[35] That the major attacks carried out in Western Europe post-9/11 (i.e., Madrid, London, Paris, Brussels) have been caused by what in the mainstream research literature on terrorism are referred to as "homegrown" terrorists has brought oil to the fire.[36] The threat of Islamic violence is everywhere and the enemy is among "us."[37]

As is well known, when white ultra-nationalists and fascists commit what are usually labeled terrorist acts when committed by Muslim citizens, their identity is never reduced to Scandinavian-ness, British-ness, or French-ness. They are never portrayed as radical or fundamentalist interpreters of nationalism as jihadi militants are portrayed as the twisted interpreters of Islam. Regardless of what history withholds, they are commonly pathologized as

[33] See Stuart Croft, *Securitising Islam* (Cambridge: Cambridge University Press, 2012); June Edmunds, "The 'New' Barbarians: Governmentality, securitization and Islam in Western Europe," *Contemporary Islam* 6(1) (2012), 67–84; Luca Mavelli, "Between Normalisation and Exception: The securitisation of Islam and the construction of the secular subject," *Millennium: Journal of International Studies* 41(2), 2013, 159–181.

[34] Per-Erik Nilsson, "Where's Charlie,," in *The Cambridge Companion to Religion and Terrorism*, ed. James R. Lewis (Cambridge: Cambridge University Press, 2017).

[35] Homi Bhabha, *The Location of Culture* (London and New York: Routledge, 2004).

[36] Lorne L. Dawson, "The Study of New Religious Movements and the Radicalization of Home-Grown Terrorists: Opening a dialogue," *Terrorism and Political Violence* 22 (1) (2009), 1–21.

[37] Liz Fekete and Frances Webber, "Foreign Nationals, Enemy Penology and the Criminal Justice System,"*Race & Class* 51(4) (2010), 1–25.

individuals foreign to the European nationalist ethos. The association of radicalism, violence, and terrorism with Islam appears so deeply rooted that when violent attacks happen, even academic and public experts who ought to be well-read in the statistics of political violence jump to unfounded conclusions.[38] Racist and fascist activists "home-grown terrorists" have even brought this element into the calculation when targeting Muslim immigrants.[39]

Now, if the non-Muslim individual's violence is pathologized, the liberal democratic state's violence is rationalized. Herein lies one of the most important aspects concerning the social and political functions of the discourse of Islamic terrorism. By simultaneously delegitimizing the violence of the "Muslim other" and pathologizing and/or rationalizing "our" violence, serious attempts to understand, explain, and remedy the causes of this violence appear futile. To quote Phil Scraton:

> To strike terror into the heart of an identifiable community is to frighten people so deeply that they lose trust and confidence in all aspects of routine daily life. Yet, to demonise perpetrators, to represent their humaneness as monstrousness, creates and sustains a climate within which a deeper understanding of historical, political and cultural contexts is inhibited and is replaced by an all-consuming will to vengeance.[40]

[38] See, e.g., the immediate responses to Anders Bering Breivik's attacks in Siv Sandvik and Oddvin Aune, "Terroreksperter tror Al-Qaida står bakom," *NRK* July 22, 2011, accessed March 24, 2016, www.nrk.no/norge/tror-al-qaida-star-bak-1.7723020.

[39] See Mattias Gardell, *Raskrigaren* (Stockholm: Leopard Förlag).

[40] Phil Scraton, "Witnessing 'Terror,' Anticipating 'War,'" in *Beyond September 9/11: An anthology of discent*, ed. Phil Scraton (London and Sterling: Pluto Press, 2002), 3.

That lessons learned from the Bush administration's declaration of a global war against terror have led to the institutionalization of a global state of emergency with grave violations of human rights and international law is well known by now.[41] Still, this will to vengeance that Scraton refers to coupled with emotional responses seem to guide state officials when talking about terrorism. This was visible not least after the Paris attacks November 13, 2015, when President François Hollande and PM Manuel Valls in unison declared a war against terrorism and promised to strike ruthlessly, home and abroad.[42] In a time of perpetual and escalating fear, the importance of studying the discourse of Islamic terrorism should not be underestimated. As Fred Halliday argues, words can "kill, and promote fear, hatred and misunderstanding"; this is why "they need to be studied, challenged and controlled."[43] What is at stake is the very foundation of the democratic nation-state's rule of law.

Outline of the Element

This Element is a critical introduction to the field of terrorism studies. It is a synthesis of previous literature in the field, and especially so on mainstream terrorism studies and critical terrorism studies. Given the limited range of this Element, generous references will guide the reader to further and in-depth reading. Some empirical material and field notes from other related research projects of my own will be discussed in the Element. Drawing on the work of Michel Foucault, the major aim of the Element is to problematize the discourse of Islamic terrorism. A problematizing analysis is not simply a matter of

---

[41] See Didier Bigo and Anastassia Tsoukala, eds., *Terror, Insecurity and Liberty: Illiberal practices of liberal regimes after 9/11* (London and New York: Routledge, 2008).

[42] See Nilsson, "Where's."

[43] Fred Halliday, *Shocked and Awed: A dictionary of the war on terror* (Berkeley: University of California Press, 2011), xv.

analyzing the presentation of Islamic terrorism as a preexisting object, nor is it the analysis of an object that does not exist. Rather, the analysis is a way to understand "the discursive and non-discursive practices that transform something to an object of thought and make it part of relations of truth and false."[44] Regarding Islamic violence, the aim of the Element is thus not to provide an answer about what it is but, instead, to provide the reader with an account of the emergence of Islamic terrorism as a problem of inquiry and, moreover, with theoretical tools to unpack truth claims about it. This means that I approach Islamic terrorism as an object construed by discourse and that there are no unmediated ways to understand what it is.[45] This does not, of course, mean that I seek to endorse, justify, glorify, or defend "Islamic" violence, nor does it mean that I am not concerned about the sort of violence this Element talks about. While this might appear as a self-evident statement, researchers working in the field have been arrested for having downloaded material from al-Qaida, which, as David Miller and Tom Mills point out, highlights "the emerging and ongoing difficulties of teaching about 'terrorism' and political violence in the current climate."[46]

A second aim is to provide for a critical overview of the events and theories that make out the epistemic field of the discourse of Islamic terrorism in

---

[44] Michel Foucault, "Le souci de la vérité,," in *Dits et écrits II* (Paris: Gallimard, 2001), 1489.

[45] Ondrej Ditrych, *Tracing the Discourses of Terrorism: Identity, genealogy and the state* (Basingstoke: Palgrave Macmillan); Michel Foucault, *L'archéologie du savoir* (Paris: Gallimard, 1969); Ernesto Laclau and Chantal Mouffe, *Hegemony and Socialist Strategy: Towards a radical democratic politics* (London: Verso, 2001); Jacob Torfing, *New Theories of Discourse: Laclau, Mouffe, and Žižek* (London: Blackwell Publishers, 1999).

[46] David Miller and Tom Mills, "Introduction: Teaching and researching terrorism – pressures and practice," *Critical Studies on Terrorism* 4(3) (2011), 389 [389–392].

the European Union (EU) and its member states.[47] A final aim is to propose a diagnosis of some of the political and social consequences that the discourse of Islamic terrorism has in the EU and its member states as well as constructive ways to think about Islamic terrorism and political violence in general. It is hoped that the Element will function as an informed introduction for any student of the topics discussed here, be they university students, journalists, politicians, activists, or the general reader.

The Element is structured around a critical discussion of three central tropes in the academic discourse on Islamic terrorism in Europe: terrorism, radicalization, and counterterrorism. This surely does not cover the whole academic discourse on Islamic terrorism in Europe but, as I argue, it captures the most significant traits of it. In the first section, I discuss the axiomatic trope of the discourse – terrorism. This means that I briefly present the emergence of terrorism as an object of study in Western academia and the discursive predicaments involved when classifying terrorism as Islamic. The section is meant to function as a general introduction to the two dominant schools within terrorism studies. In the second section, I bring to the fore the emergence of the trope radicalization and examine its overarching ontology and epistemology in mainstream and critical approaches to the study of terrorism. Section three discusses the intersections of academic and political discourses on Islamic terrorism by examining the trope counter-radicalization as well as deradicalization that emerged as central aspects of counterterrorism measures. The discussion is related to broader counterterrorist measurements taken by the EU and its member states. The final section is a critical discussion of the previous sections. Here I draw on what I refer to as radical approaches to the study of

---

[47] Europe is, of course, not equal to the EU, and focus could also be turned toward the Balkans, Russia, and Turkey. This is, however, rarely done in the literature on Islamic terrorism in Europe, wherefore I have left this out.

terrorism to examine the political and social functions of the academic and political discourse of Islamic terrorism as well as some of the political and social risks involved with the expanding counter-radicalization/terrorist apparatuses.

"Holy Rage"

It is has become a truism in mainstream literature on terrorism to state that the category of "terrorism" is notoriously difficult to define, just as it has become a truism in critical literature on terrorism to state that this statement is a truism.[48] Like many other central categories in the human and social sciences, such as democracy, ideology, culture, and religion, terrorism is a contested category whose meaning is not given beforehand.[49] As Richard Jackson points out, similar to these other categories, terrorism has become a commonsensical part of the narratives we tell about who we are in more general terms.[50] However, that the meaning of the category of terrorism is both contested and over-shadowed by commonsensical statements does not mean that it cannot be defined. A study conducted as early as 1988 found that no fewer than 109 definitions of terrorism were in use (i.e., 109 possible ways of defining

---

[48] E.g., Richard Jackson, Marie Breen Smyth, and Jeroen Gunning, "Critical Terrorism Studies: Framing a new research agenda," in *Critical Terrorism Studies. A new research agenda*, eds., Richard Jackson, Marie Breen Smyth, and Jeroen Gunning (London and New York: Routledge, 2009), 217 [216–236]; Leonard Weinberg, Ami Pedahzur, and Sivan Hirsch-Hoffler, "The Challenges of Conceptualizing Terrorism," *Terrorism and Political Violence* 16(4) (2004), 777–794.

[49] Gallie, W. B, "Essentially Contested Concepts." *Proceedings of the Aristotelian Society* 56 (1955), 167–198.

[50] Jackson, "Constructing," 395.

terrorism).[51] A more recent survey lists 250 definitions.[52] What is often implicitly suggested in the statement that terrorism cannot be defined is that one common definition cannot be agreed upon, which is a matter other than the definition itself. But even this aspect of the question of definition does not differ from other central categories. First of all, the desire to define is a treacherous one. Definitions are often assumed to merely label imagined universal phenomena such as terrorism. In this regard, the desire to define becomes a quest for the all-encompassing final definition – a quest mimicking that in the natural sciences. This brings up a second issue. The assumption that a final definition can be achieved at all is based on the idea that somehow scholars could retract *themselves* from the workings of power and ideology and reach objective, rational, and universal definitions of the order of things. Finally, the quest for definitions does not take into consideration the performative aspect of definitions, that is, that labeling, naming, and classifying are intricate parts of the game of knowledge *production*.[53] When it comes to the category "Islamic," as in Islamic terrorism, there appears to be less confusion since few mainstream scholars seem to ponder upon its definition. The category Islamic appears self-explicatory and in this sense it is what brings stability to the meaning of the category terrorism. Islamic terrorism has come to denote a specific form of

---

[51] Alex P. Schmid and Albert J. Jongman, *Political Terrorism: A new guide to actors, authors, concepts, data bases, theories, and literature* (New Brunswick, NJ: Transaction Publishers, 2005), 5–6.

[52] Alex P. Schmid, ed., *The Routledge Handbook of Terrorism Research* (London and New York: Routledge), 39.

[53] See further Andrew Barry, Thomas Osborne, and Nikolas Rose, eds, *Foucault and Political Reason: Liberalism, neo-liberalism, and rationalities of government* (Chicago: University of Chicago Press, 1996).

religious violence that is particularly bad or evil, something that has become a normalized part of the discourse of Islamic terrorism post-9/11.[54]

In this section, I present an overview of how terrorism and especially Islamic terrorism emerged as objects for academic inquiry and, moreover, the various approaches to Islamic terrorism in the acclaimed dominant schools of thought within the field of terrorism studies – mainstream and critical approaches to terrorism. Critical scholars usually name these approaches mainstream terrorism studies (MTS) and critical terrorism studies (CTS).[55] The borders dividing these schools of thought are sometimes vague, and there are conflicting ideas about what terrorism is within each school. I maintain these divisions because they help structure the field of terrorism studies after a number of ontological and epistemological premises. More precisely, mainstream scholars tend to define terrorism as violent acts and/or an ideology by non-state actors whose main targets are civilians – at least that is what critical scholars argue that they do. Critical terrorism scholars often share the ontological premise of mainstream scholars, most notably by arguing that terrorism is an observable phenomenon. However, although they share some ontological premises with the mainstream field, they are critical toward its epistemology, most notably its alleged state-centrism and poor research methods.

[54] See William T. Cavanaugh, *The Myth of Religious Violence: Secular ideology and the roots of modern conflict* (Oxford: Oxford University Press, 2009).

[55] Critical scholars also refer to the mainstream field as orthodox terrorism studies. For more comprehensive studies, see Martha Crenshaw, "Terrorism Research: The record," *International Interactions* 40(4) (2014), 556–567; Richard Jackson, Lee Jarvis, Jeroen Gunning, and Marie Breen Smyth, *Terrorism: A critical introduction* (New York: Palgrave Macmillan, 2011); Stampnitzky, *Disciplining*; Mikkel Thorup, *An Intellectual History of Terror* (London and New York: Routledge, 2010).

The Progressive Terrorist

Terrorism has, in its brief history as an analytical category in academia, been contested. Well before 9/11, Mihalis Halkides asked, "[i]s terrorism what we have been led to believe?" He continued, "[c]oncerns about terrorism reached their peak between the late 1970s and mid 1980s."[56] Halkides, of course, could not have foreseen the expansion of his field of study during the coming decade. Today it appears impossible to think about a world without terrorism, however we choose to define or not define it, since it is at once everywhere and nowhere. As I show in the coming sections, terrorism as a category has its own contingent history, and it is indeed a history in the making.

In the MTS literature on terrorism, religious terrorism appears as the exemplary case. As Walter Laqueur suggests, religious terrorism has been a part of human history for a good couple of millennia: "[R]eligion has always been a main feature of terrorism; the Sicari, the Assassins, and the Indian secret societies practicing thugee were religious sects, and have given us the words 'zealot', 'assassin', and 'thug.'"[57] Making a statement of this sort is to suggest that terrorism is a phenomenon with an essential universal meaning that can be found throughout history. However, the category of terrorism seems to have emerged and entered political speech (in Latin and German languages) with the French Revolution in 1789, although its meaning differed somewhat from that of today. To Maximilien de Robespierre, who spoke about "terror" and not "terrorism," it referred to "nothing more than justice prompt, severe,

---

[56] Mihalis Halkides, "How Not to Study Terrorism," *Peace Review* 7(3–4) (1995), 253 [253–260].

[57] Walter Laqueur, *The New Terrorism: Fanaticism and the arms of mass destruction* (New York and Oxford: Oxford University Press, 1999), 127.

inflexible."[58] Although this definition is not far from how Al-Qaida or ISIS makes use of the category, it is far removed from mainstream definitions of terror(ism). The important thing to note here is that Robespierre spoke on behalf of the new republic, that is, the state. In other words, terror was a tool to be used by the state to inflict justice. During the course of the Revolution, moreover, terror seems to have developed from being a mere tool of justice to become a form of government, like tyranny, monarchy, or despotism. However, as argued by Verena Erlenbush, "it quickly underwent a number of transformations that complicate an understanding of terrorism both as a particular form of violence and in terms of state and non-state violence."[59] For example, terrorism came to be understood "as a philosophical reflection on normative principles of political organisation" thus designating "political commitments, like republicanism, populism or royalism."[60] The important thing to note here is that terror and terrorism are categories born in the same era as other modernist categories and concepts including male (universal) suffrage and human rights, where, as Erlenbusch concludes, for progressive thinkers and activists it surely must have been "desirable to be a terrorist."[61] The reigning idea of today that terrorism has to do with non-state actors did not take root until the middle of the nineteenth century.[62]

---

[58] Quoted in Jørgen Staun, "When, How and Why Elites Frame Terrorists: A Wittgensteinian analysis of terror and radicalisation," *Critical Studies on Terrorism* 3(3) (2010), 405 [403–420].

[59] Verena Erlenbusch, "Terrorism and Revolutionary Violence: The emergence of terrorism in the French Revolution," *Critical Studies on Terrorism* 8(2) (2015), 194 [193–210].

[60] Erlenbusch, "Terrorism," 198. [61] Erlenbusch, "Terrorism," 200.

[62] Verena Erlenbusch, "How (Not) to Study Terrorism," *Critical Review of International Social and Political Philosophy* 17(4) (2014), 482 [470–491].

Terrorism Becomes Mainstream

The categories of terror and terrorism are thus no newcomers to political speech. The contemporary discourse of terrorism sees its formation during the 1970s and its institutionalization as a proper academic field during the 1980s.[63] This is achieved through the publication of the journals *Studies in Terrorism in Conflict* (1977) and *Terrorism and Political Violence* (1989), as well as through publications by research centers such as the Research and Development Corporation (RAND) and the St Andrews Centre for Studies in Terrorism and Political Violence (CSPTV).[64] Until the 1970s, there was virtually no systematic work on terrorism,[65] and acts today classified as terrorism were considered to be cases of insurgency, guerrilla warfare, banditism, rebellion, and revolutionary acts. One of the few resemblances with today's usage is how terrorism was deployed to name violent challenges to European colonial rule.[66] As Lisa Stampnitzky points out, the United States referred to airplane hijacking as "air piracy" and treated it as "a routine domestic criminal matter."[67] In this regard, terror or terrorism was understood as "but one stage in a broader process of insurgency or revolution – a stage through which groups could pass without permanently tainting their reputations."[68]

From Piracy to Terrorism

During the 1970s, a large number of studies of terrorism began to be published. Conservative Anglo-American scholars with close ties to Western governments

---

[63] For an account of earlier usages see Ditrych, *Tracing*.

[64] Jackson et al., *Terrorism*, 10. [65] Crenshaw, "Terrorism."

[66] Adrian Guelke, "Great Whites, Paedophiles and Terrorists: The need for critical thinking in a new age of fear," *Critical Studies on Terrorism* 1(1) (2008), 17 [17–25].

[67] Stampnitzky, *Disciplining*, 2. [68] Stampnitzky, *Disciplining*, 52.

dominated the emerging field.[69] The institutionalization of terrorism studies coincides with a shift in US policy: the Reagan administration's focus on hard-line measures and the emergence of "counterterrorism" from the preceding Carter administration's focus on "human rights."[70] The object of inquiry here changes from being considered a tactic of war or, more precisely, an illegitimate war terror legitimizing extralegal retaliation. As Stampnitzky explains:

> The reframing of terrorism as a war was not just a discursive shift; it also shaped how the Reagan administration (and the subsequent administrations of George H. W. Bush and Bill Clinton) concretely responded to the problem. While the governance of terrorism in the 1970s was dominated by the logics of law, risk, and crisis management, in the 1980s a military logic came to the fore. But, in contrast to the pre-emptive "war on terror" that would arise after 9/11, this first war on terror was driven by a logic of retaliation, in which military counterterrorism strikes were akin to punishment for a crime. This reframing of terrorism as war was an explicit technique of delegitimization: terrorism was redefined as outside the laws of war and crime, and thus illegitimate in both means and ends.[71]

During the 1970s and 1980s, terrorism emerges as an area of expertise and, together with newly crowned experts and publications, the period sees an outpouring of definitions of terrorism, some more precise than others. Laqueur, for

---

[69] E.g., Yonah Alexander, Paul Bremer, Ray Cline, Martha Crenshaw, Brian Jenkins, Walter Laqueur, Paul Leventhal, Ariel Merari, Edward Mickolus, Benjamin Netanyahu, Robert O. Slater, and Paul Wilkinson. See Halkides, "How," 253–254.

[70] Halkides, "How," 253. [71] Stampnitzky, *Disciplining*, 110.

example, states that terrorism, while being hard to describe, is still easily recognizable: "It has been said that it resembles pornography: difficult to describe and define, but easy to recognize when one sees it."[72] Laqueur has also been a strong advocate for the theory of the crazy or insane terrorist:

> Madness, especially paranoia, plays a role in contemporary terrorism. Not all paranoiacs are terrorists, but all terrorists believe in conspiracies by the powerful, hostile forces and suffer from some form of delusion and persecution mania … madness plays an important role, even if many are reluctant to acknowledge it.[73]

Commonsensical and imprecise ways of approaching terrorism of this sort have been matched by a plethora of other definitions. One is the still-influential definition of terrorism as a theater: "It is the message that makes terrorism. There is a sender (the terrorist), a message generator (the victim) and a receiver (the public). Also, in order for a violent act to become terroristic, it needs an audience."[74] There have also been attempts to unite the field around a common definition. For example, in 1988, Alex Schmid and Albert Jongman published an "Academic Consensus Definition" construed on the basis of 50 scholars' answers to a questionnaire:

---

[72] Walter Laqueur and Yonah Alexander, ed., *The Terrorism Reader* (New York: Meridian, 1987), 380.

[73] Walter Laqueur, "Left, Right and Beyond: The changing face of terror," in *How Did This Happen? Terrorism and the new war*, eds. J. Hoge and G. Rose (New York: Public Affairs, 2001), 80 [71–82].

[74] Alex P. Schmid and Janny de Graaf, *Violence as Communication: Insurgent terrorism and the Western news media* (London: Sage Publications, 1982), 15.

Terrorism is an anxiety-inspiring method of repeated violent action, employed by (semi-) clandestine individual, group, or state actors, for idiosyncratic, criminal, or political reasons, whereby – in contrast to assassination – the direct targets of violence are not the main targets. The immediate human victims of violence are generally chosen randomly (targets of opportunity) or selectively (representative or symbolic targets) from a target population, and serve as message generators. Threat- and violence-based communication processes between terrorist (organization), (imperilled) victims, and main targets are used to manipulate the main target (audience(s)), turning it into a target of terror, a target of demands, or a target of attention, depending on whether intimidation, coercion, or propaganda is primarily sought.[75]

While this definition covers an impressive number of activities, it both inflates and reduces the category to analytical incoherencies due to its internal contradictions: for example, targets are chosen *randomly* or *selectively*. Leonard Weinberg, Ami Pedahzur, and Sivan Hirsch-Hoefler have attempted another consensus. They conclude that terrorism "is a politically motivated tactic involving the threat or use of force or violence in which the pursuit of publicity plays a significant role."[76] Yet another attempt has been proposed by David Whittaker, who argues that terrorism is first of all "ineluctably about power: the pursuit of power, the acquisition of power, and the use of power to achieve

---

[75] Schmid and Jongman, *Political*, 28.

[76] Leonard Weinberg, Ami Pedahzur, and Sivan Hirsch-Hoefler, "The Challenges of Conceptualizing Terrorism," *Terrorism and Political Violence* 16(4) (2004), 786 [777–794].

political change," which leads to the conclusion that terrorism "is thus violence – or equally important, the threat of violence – used and directed in pursuit of, or in service of, a political aim."[77]

Given the disparity of definitions even among those who seek consensus definitions, it is, as Martha Crenshaw concludes, "thus necessary to recognize that an important aspect of terrorism is its social construction, which is relative to time and place, thus to historical context. It is not a neutral descriptive term."[78] This is visible not least in how early terrorism scholarship selectively designated non-US-friendly regimes and groups as terrorists, while using other categories, such as "insurgents" and "freedom fighters," for US-friendly actors.[79] Similarly, as Halkides notes, in Europe the category seems largely to have been reserved for "leftist guerrillas" and "separatist movements" but not for "right-wing groups … including racists, neo-fascists, and paramilitary groups" and "right-wing dictatorships."[80]

Earthquake Machines and Asteroids

During the late 1980s and early 1990s, MTS scholars started to focus on what is perceived as a new yet simultaneously old phenomenon.[81] In 1998, Laqueur stated that while politics had come to replace the thousand-years-old religiously motivated terrorism, "a worldwide resurgence of radical religious

---

[77] David J. Whittaker, *The Terrorism Reader* (London: Routledge, 2012), 9.

[78] Martha Crenshaw, "Thoughts on Relating Terrorism to Historical Contexts," in *Terrorism in Context*, ed. Martha Crenshaw (University Park: Pennsylvania University Press, 1995), 8.

[79] Halkides, "How," 254.   [80] Halkides, "How," 255.

[81] E.g., Bruce Hoffman, "'Holy Terror': The implications of terrorism motivated by the religious imperative," RAND (1993), accessed February 23, 2016, www.rand.org/content/dam/rand/pubs/papers/2007/P7834.pdf.

movements" was in the making.[82] This is the basis of the theory of "new terrorism," which by and large coincides with the general "return of religion" theory within the then humanities and social sciences.[83] In 1995, Magnus Ranstorp stated that "a surge of religious fanaticism has manifested itself in spectacular acts of terrorism across the globe."[84] This terrorism, exemplified by the Japanese Aum Shinrikyo, al-Jama'a al-Islamiyya, and white supremacism in the United States, we learn, is different from its predecessor. Not only is it "far afield from the traditionally violent Middle East," it is more lethal, indiscriminate and, from the perpetrators' point of view, "sanctioned, [or] even mandated, by God."[85]

The new religiously motivated terrorism, that is mostly taken to mean Islamic terrorism, differs in three aspects: its ideology, its strategy, and its end goals. Regarding ideology, Ranstorp states: "Unlike secular counterparts, religious terrorists are, by their very nature, largely motivated by religion."[86] While a theory suggesting that religious terrorists are religiously motivated might come as less of a surprise, it is noticeable that the statement is made

[82] Laqueur, *The New*, 127. Also see Alex P. Schmid, "Frameworks for Conceptualizing Terrorism," *Terrorism and Political Violence* 16(2) (2004), 210 [197–221].

[83] On the new terrorism theory, see Bruce Hoffman, "The Emergence of the New Terrorism," in *The New Terrorism*, eds., A. Tan and K. Ramakrishna (Singapore: Eastern Universities Press, 2002), 30–49; Mark Juergensmeyer, "Understanding the New Terrorism," *Current History* 99 (2000), 158–163; Laqueur, *The New*; Ian O. Lesser, Bruce Hoffman, John Arquilla, David Ronfeldt, and Michele Zanini, eds., *Countering the New Terrorism* (Santa Monica: RAND, 1999); Peter R. Neumann, *Old and New Terrorism* (Cambridge: Polity Press, 2009). On the return of religion theory, see James A. Beckford, "The Return of Public Religion? A Critical Assessment of a Popular Claim," *Nordic Journal of Religion* 23(2) (2010), 121–136.

[84] Magnus Ranstorp, "Terrorism in the Name of Religion," *Journal of International Affairs* 50(1) (1996), 43 [41–62].

[85] Ranstorp, "Terrorism," 43–44. [86] Ranstorp, "Terrorism," 44.

without defining what religion supposedly is. That religion is prone to violence appears as age-old wisdom. Alex Schmid quotes sixteenth-century philosopher Blaise Pascal to prove this theory: "Men never do evil so openly and contentedly as when they do it from religious conviction."[87] Mark Juergensmeyer, one of the most influential scholars on religion and violence, proposes that religion is fundamental when it comes to legitimizing terrorist acts since "it provides images of cosmic war that allow activists to believe that they waging spiritual scenarios."[88] Drawing on Juergensmeyer, Lorne Dawson concludes that "religiously inspired violence differs from all other forms in that the acts of violence constitute ritual performances with a symbolic significance."[89]

The "cosmic war" aside, Ranstorp concludes that religious terrorists "are also driven by day-to-day practical considerations" and that this "makes it difficult for the *general* observer to separate and distinguish between the political and the religious sphere of these terrorist groups," which is nowhere more clear than "in Muslim terrorist groups as religion and politics cannot be separated in Islam."[90] In this logic, Islam and religiously or politically engaged Muslims are a poor fit with the secular West. As suggested by Ayla Schbley, democracy is "to most contemporary Muslim nations, as alien to them as pork rinds."[91] Laqeueur similarly states, without any proper

---

[87] Schmid, "Frameworks," 211.

[88] Mark Juergensmeyer, *Terror in the Mind of God: The global rise of religious violence* (Berkeley: University of California Press, 2000), xi.

[89] Lorne L. Dawson, "The Study of New Religious Movements and the Radicalization of Home-Grown Terrorists: Opening a dialogue," *Terrorism and Political Violence* 22 (1) (2009), 1–21.

[90] Ranstorp, "Terrorism," 44.

[91] Ayla Schbley, "Religious Terrorism, the Media, and International Islamization Terrorism: Justifying the unjustifiable," *Studies in Conflict & Terrorism* 27 (2004), 208.

analysis, that the "aggressive element in radical Islam," is a "Holy Rage" that is stronger than in other religions.[92]

A holy rage leading to a cosmic war is not the only particularity of this new terrorism; it differs in strategy and organization from its predecessor. The fear of terrorists using the strategy of getting weapons of mass destruction (WMD) becomes common during this period. Ian Lesser discusses these "troubling new dimensions," which include "the potential for terrorist action on U.S. territory and terrorist use of weapons of mass destruction – nuclear, chemical, biological, and radiological."[93] Laqueur does not stop with weapons already known to man but adds to the list of WMDs an "earthquake machine" and "artificial meteors."[94] Commenting on the idea of terrorism as a theater for communicating a message, Laquer concludes that the new terrorism is terrorism for its own sake. The new terrorism is "indiscriminate in the choice of its victims" and "its aim is no longer to conduct propaganda but to effect maximum destruction."[95] As such, Laqueur adds, the new terrorism is highly unpredictable and that "[s]urprises might always be ahead."[96] Indeed, the surprises awaiting us might even be humanity's total annihilation. "This new terrorism," Laqueur states, intends to "liquidate all satanic forces," which, in "its maddest, most extreme form," may lead to "the destruction of all life on earth, as the ultimate punishment for mankind's crimes."[97]

The new terrorists are also thought to differ in their organizational structure. According to Peter Neumann, who prefers to talk about old*er* and new*er* terrorism, terrorism is a social phenomenon that "consists of small

[92] Laqueur, *The New*, 128.

[93] Ian O. Lesser, "Introduction," in *Countering*, Lesser et al., eds., 1.

[94] Laqueur, *The New*, 264.

[95] Walter Laqueur, *No End to War* (New York: Continuum, 2003), 9.

[96] Laqueur, *No End*, 10. [97] Laqueur, *The New*, 81.

conspiracies (structure) aiming to achieve political objectives (aim) through symbolic acts of extra-normal violence (method)."[98] The new terrorists, then, have supposedly "changed their structures from hierarchy to network," where "religion has come to be a prominent source of their aims and ideologies," and, finally, "their methods have shifted towards the application of more excessive and indiscriminate forms of violence."[99] These core precepts of the theory of new terrorism have been widely popularized by scholars, journalists, and self-avowed and mediatized experts post-9/11.[100]

The politically sensitive question of terrorism has also led to moralizing and taboos. The category of terrorism has come to designate "the legitimacy of political authority," as stated by Crenshaw.[101] It has developed into a pejorative term used by scholars and states to categorize enemies and unwanted elements.[102] Considering the contemporary academic arena, in 2013 the much-renowned MTS journal *Terrorism and Political Violence* published an entire issue whose main purpose was to delegitimize those scholars questioning the accuracy of the (Islamic) discourse on terrorism. James Hopkins has analyzed the issue and questions the normative approach: "The present issue's main goal is to point toward a general approach to the question of why violence and terror hold such a

---

[98] Neumann, *Old*, 16. [99] Neumann, *Old*, 16.

[100] E.g., Peter Bergen, *United States of Jihad: Investigating America's homegrown terrorists* (New York: Crown Publishing Group, 2016); Sam Harris, *The End of Faith: Religion, terror, and the future of religion* (London: Simon & Schuster, 2006); Christofer Hitchens, *God Is Not Great: How religion is poisoning everything* (London: Atlantic Books, 2007); Charles Kimball, *When Religion Becomes Evil* (New York: HarperCollins, 2008); Melanie Philips, *Londonistan: Britain's terror state from within* (New York: Encounter Books, 2006).

[101] Crenshaw (1995, 9)

[102] Thomas Mathiesen, "Expanding the Concept of Terrorism," in *Beyond September 11: An anthology of dissent*, ed. Phil Scraton (London and Sterling, VA: Pluto Press, 2002), 85–93.

powerful appeal for intellectuals."[103] In the issue, Richard Landes states, "today, we have intellectuals … running interference for Islamism," and that their actions potentially give the terrorists "a cognitive victory in which its targets in the West are kept in the dark about its real intentions."[104] Furthermore, this support for terrorism is portrayed as an existential threat, as he asserts the danger of "cultural, even civilizational suicide."[105] While no empirical evidence for these accusations is provided and they could be dismissed as being nothing more than accusations based on politics, statements of this sort remain problematic. As Hopkins argues: "To accuse someone of supporting terrorism … is also a serious claim to make, with real consequences that follow. So, what is immediately striking is that the special issue contains no discussion of the ethics of making such an accusation."[106]

No Pens for Hire

MTS is not a homogenous field. While scholars classified under this category share certain ontological and epistemological assumptions, there has been and still are debates concerning the definition, the nature, and the efficacy of terrorism and how to defeat it. Even if a large proportion of leading scholars have had close ties to government officials, this is not to say that everybody is working as a pen for hire. In fact, after 9/11, 698 US-based scholars made a public declaration

[103] Helena Rimon and Ron Schleifer, "Who Will Guard the Guardians? Introduction to the Special Issue on the Intellectuals and Terror: A Fatal Attraction," *Terrorism and Political Violence* 25(4) (2013), 511 [511–517].

[104] Richard Landes, "From Useful Idiot to Useful Infidel: Meditations on the folly of 21st-century 'intellectuals,'" *Terrorism and Political Violence* 25(4) (2013), 622 [621–634].

[105] Landes, "From," 622.

[106] James Hopkins, "Psychologically Disturbed and on the Side of the Terrorists: The delegitimisation of critical intellectuals in terrorism and political violence," *Critical Studies on Terrorism* 7(2) (2014), 297 [297–312].

bringing into question US policy. While they "applaud the Bush Administration for its initial focus on destroying al-Qaida bases in Afghanistan," they nevertheless state, "the current American policy centered around the war in Iraq is the most misguided one since the Vietnam period."[107] Moreover, as a counterbalance to the theory of new terrorism, scholars working with a more rationalist approach to terrorism have sought to debunk several of the foundations of the theory. One of the most influential in this regard is Robert Pape, who has conducted quantitative and qualitative studies of virtually all listed terrorist attacks since the 1970s for which suicide has been the technique employed. His conclusion is that "what over 95% of all suicide terrorist attacks before 2004 had in common was a strategic goal: to compel a democratic state to withdraw combat forces that are threatening territory that the terrorists prize."[108] Instead of religion explaining suicide missions, Pape concludes that the "bottom line, then, is that suicide terrorism is mainly a strategic response to foreign occupation with important, but limited, coercive power."[109] Pape, moreover, questions the particularly murderous fury of Islamic terrorists. As he says, "if religious fanaticism or any ideology was driving the threat, we would expect a spread of more or less proportionately scattered attacks around the globe or," he adds, "we are observing nearly the opposite of random."[110] This does not mean, however, that Pape abandons earlier explicatory models for suicide terrorism. On an individual level, as Claire Lyness has remarked, Pape holds that suicide bombers are the epitome

---

[107] Security Scholars for a Sensible Foreign Policy, "Time for a Change of Course: An open letter to the American people," October 12, 2004, accessed February 15, 2016, www.informationclearinghouse.info/article7070.htm.

[108] Robert A. Pape and James K. Feldman, *Cutting the Fuse. The Explosion of Global Suicide Terrorism and How to Stop It* (Chicago and London: The University of Chicago Press, 2012), 9.

[109] Pape and Feldman, *Cutting*, 25. [110] Pape and Feldman, *Cutting*, 28.

of "the rationality of irrationality."[111] Nonetheless, criticism from within and without MTS has led several scholars to revisit previous research and old assumptions.[112]

Regardless, the verdict on the mainstream field by scholars within the critical field is clear. Joseba Zulaika deplores the inner-disciplinary, narrow-minded, and moralistic underpinnings of MTS, which, according to Zulaika, have led to "a position of intellectual and moral retreat from everything we have learned from anthropology, history, and psychoanalysis."[113] Michael Stohl concludes, "the damage that the new terrorism thesis caused in the wars and other measures undertaken to defeat the falsely identified" have been "devastating."[114] How, then, have these more critically inclined scholars responded to this alleged intellectual morass?

The Critical Approach

In 2008, the journal *Critical Studies of Terrorism* was launched.[115] It quickly became a forum for critical scholars as well as a major step toward the institutionalization of CTS. Some of the prominent and most cited scholars within the field are Jeroen Gunning, Richard Jackson, Marie Breen Smyth, and Joseba Zulaika. CTS started as a reaction, as Jackson puts it, to the "[l]ack of critical

---

[111] Claire Lyness, "Governing the Suicide Bomber: Reading terrorism studies as governmentality," *Critical Studies on Terrorism* 7(1) (2014), XX [79–96].

[112] See Jackson et al., *Terrorism*, 15.

[113] Joseba Zulaika, *Terrorism: The self-fulfilling prophecy* (Chicago: University of Chicago Press, 2009).

[114] Michael Stohl, "Don't Confuse Me with the Facts: Knowledge claims and terrorism," *Critical Studies on Terrorism* 5(1) (2012), 47 [31–49]. Also see Halkides, "How," 253.

[115] The journal was preceded by symposiums and several publications. See for example *European Political Science* 6(3) (2007).

literature that falls outside of the mainstream frame."[116] Although scholars had been publishing critical research on terrorism well before 2008,[117] they were not participating as legitimate voices within the field of terrorism studies.[118] One of the main preoccupations for these critical scholars is to understand how terrorism, "a comparatively minor form of violence responsible for the deaths of a few thousand people every year globally," can generate "such a vast amount of intellectual, cultural, political, legal and security activity," considering that the number of deaths is "dwarfed by those killed through war, insurgency, repression, poverty, disease and global warming, among others."[119]

CTS has without doubt had an influence on the mainstream field and scholars from both camps have co-published work with the ambition of developing more theoretically astute and empirically grounded research.[120] Notwithstanding, the impact of CTS in the general field of terrorism studies is contested. For example, while to Eric Herring the impact indeed appears important, it is also moderate: "Up to now CTS has mainly sought to challenge the narratives and descriptions propagated under the rubric of the War on Terror."[121] This section will bring some clarity to what degree CTS is

---

[116] Richard Jackson, Marie Breen Smyth, and Jeroen Gunning, "Introduction: The case for critical terrorism studies," in Jackson et al., *Critical*, 1 [1–13].

[117] E.g., Chomsky, Noam, and Edward S. Herman, *The Political Economy of Human Rights, Volume I: The Washington Connection and Third World Fascism* (Nottingham: Spokesman, 1979); Edward Said, "The Essential Terrorist," in *Blaming the Victims: Spurious scholarship and the Palestinian question*, eds. Edward Said and Christopher Hitchens (London: Verso, 1988), 149–159.

[118] Jackson et al., *Terrorism*, 2.   [119] Jackson et al., *Terrorism*, 2.

[120] E.g., Magnus Ranstorp, "Mapping Terrorism Studies After 9/11: An academic field of old problems and new prospects," in Jackson et al., *Critical*, 17.

[121] Eric Herring and Doug Stokes, "Editors' Introduction: Bringing critical realism and historical materialism into critical terrorism studies, *Critical Studies on Terrorism* 4(1) (2011), 1–3.

equipped to move beyond the mainstream field and contribute more than simply challenging narratives and descriptions. My argument is that CTS is somewhat caught in a theoretical limbo where it appears as if CTS scholars are throwing out the bathwater of terrorism studies but keeping the baby – the category of terrorism itself. In this section, I present the major outline of CTS's ontological and epistemological premises; discuss CTS scholars' contributions to the field; and, most importantly, examine CTS scholars' definition of terrorism.

Critical Theory

One of the core principles of CTS is that it is a critical project. Being critical can entail a number of things and takes on different meanings in different theoretical schools.[122] CTS is interdisciplinary and highly eclectic. In the literature, the following are listed as analytical methodologies: "post-positivist, discourse analysis, post-structuralism, constructivism, Critical Theory, historical materialism, history, ethnography and others."[123] To this list are also added post-colonial perspectives, queer studies, and critical perspectives on religion.[124] These theoretical and methodological perspectives do indeed differ from the mainstream field, where explicit references to the epistemological and ontological foundations of research are rarely made clear. However, to what degree all these perspectives converge and are theoretically coherent is not always discussed. It also invites a number of questions: for example, to what degree is post-structuralism a methodology in the same way as discourse analysis, or to

---

[122] See e.g., Jason Glynos and David Howarth, *Logics of Critical Explanation in Social and Political Theory* (London and New York: Routledge, 2007).

[123] Jackson et al., *Terrorism*, 38. [124] Jackson et al., *Terrorism*, 77.

what degree is a Foucauldian discourse analysis compatible with discourse analysis rooted in the Frankfurt School?[125]

Within CTS, terrorism is approached ontologically as a social construction, which, as Jackson et al. put it, "has obvious implications for the way we approach it as an object of knowledge and a subject of scholarly research."[126] The obvious epistemological implications of this are, first, an examination of the "political violence" that is classified as terrorism and, second, an exploration of the "social processes" through which terrorism is constructed in time and space.[127] Putting emphasis on terrorism as a social construction means that researchers themselves are active parties, not only in the knowledge production of terrorism but also in the very construction of terrorism as an object of inquiry, which differs from the mainstream field. Harmonie Toros and Jeroen Gunning put it this way:

> Accepting that theory and knowledge are always rooted in their historical context and serve particular interests clearly places Critical Theorists in direct opposition to the traditional realist position that politics can and must be studied from a neutral objective standpoint. Indeed, it not only questions the very possibility of situating oneself outside the social world, but also asks the fundamental question of who benefits from a theory that advocates an objective neutral standpoint.[128]

[125] On methodological issues, see Torfing, *New Theories*.

[126] Jackson et al., *Terrorism*, 3. [127] Jackson et al., *Terrorism*, 3.

[128] Harmonie Toros and Jeroen Gunning, "Exploring a Critical Theory Approach to Terrorism Studies," in Jackson et al., *Critical*, 87 [87–108].

This statement echoes Foucauldian sensitivity to the intersection of power and knowledge, but it also seems to direct attention to a more explicit analysis of ideology with the stated focus on revealing who benefits from what.[129] Based on its ontological and epistemological foundation, terrorism cannot, or should not be able to, exist outside the gaze of the observer. Or, more accurately, terrorism should not be able to preexist discourse, a question I will come back to. Nonetheless, Jackson et al. explain that "'terrorist' is not an identity like 'Amish' or 'Canadian', nor is it the case that 'once a terrorist, always a terrorist.'"[130] In other words, attributing to someone the label of "terrorist" is not a neutral and objective classification but one related to power and ideology. Now, it can be questioned to what degree any identity can exist outside the game of knowledge and power, meaning that the comparison is odd, to say the least.

For leading scholars within CTS, a normative-ethical commitment is added to their critical project. Researchers should favor "human rights, progressive politics and improving the lives of individuals and communities" by following "the dictum that the point of knowledge is not just to understand the world, but to change it for the better."[131] This means that "CTS scholars for the most part see emancipation as a process of trying to construct 'concrete utopias' by realizing the unfulfilled potential of existing structures, freeing individuals from unnecessary [sic] structural constraints and the democratization of the public sphere."[132] The ambition, then, is not only directed toward "tolerating difference" but also to enlarge "human diversity" itself.[133] The end goal is, as Jackson states, directed toward "ending avoidable [sic] human suffering."[134]

[129] Jackson et al., *Terrorism*, 35–36. [130] Jackson et al., *Terrorism*, 35–36.
[131] Jackson et al., *Terrorism*, 30–31. [132] Jackson et al., *Terrorism*, 39.
[133] Toros and Gunning, "Exploring," in Jackson et al., *Critical*, 102 [87–108].
[134] Jackson et al., "Critical," 223–224.

One important part of CTS emancipatory ambition is to include nation-states in the analysis of terrorism. While mainstream scholars have not neglected state-terror,[135] the analytical lens has rarely been turned toward liberal democracies.[136] Michel Stohl argues that "the vast majority of scholars who study terrorism today continue to ignore the etymological roots and historical employment of terrorism by the state and rarely consider the violence perpetrated by the state against its own population or those of states beyond its borders."[137] Omitting the state from any analysis of terrorism is, according to Stohl, a grave error since "it remains the case that the most persistent and successful use of terror both in the past and in the modern era has been demonstrated by governments for the purpose of creating, maintaining, and imposing order."[138] This is the case especially since the "number of victims produced by state terror is on a scale exponentially larger than that of insurgent terrorists."[139] The lack of analysis of state-terror is one thing that CTS scholars have sought to remedy, most notably by analyzing the counterproductive aspects of the war on terror, such as the US drone programs and the normalization of extralegal measures legitimized through a global state of exception.[140]

What's so Religious about Terrorism?

As the ambition of this Element is to analyze the scholarly discourse on Islamic terrorism in Europe, the contribution by CTS in the meticulous analysis of the theory of new terrorism and its epistemological and ontological foundations is particularly important. By drawing on postcolonial and critical research on religion, CTS scholars have come to challenge many prevailing truths regarding

---

[135] E.g., Laqueur, *The New*.

[136] Richard Jackson, "Unknown Knowns: The subjugated knowledge of terrorism studies," *Critical Studies on Terrorism* 5(1) (2012), 13 [11–29]

[137] Stohl, *Old*, 5–6. [138] Stohl, *Old*, 6. [139] Stohl, *Old*, 6. [140] See Zulaika, *Terrorism*.

religion, most notably Islam, that have been reproduced uncritically by many scholars within the mainstream field. The critique can be divided into two topics: the distinction between the religious and the secular, and the one-sided focus on Islamic terrorism.

CTS scholars not only question the common distinction between the religious and the secular held by mainstream scholars but also one of the most unquestioned truth claims in Western scholarship.[141] Gunning and Jackson argue that the distinction between the religious and the secular is problematic both empirically and theoretically. They argue that the notion of religious terrorism "is based on the assumption that religion is clearly definable and distinguishable from the secular and political realms" and that "the label has little meaning without further qualification, while simultaneously obscuring important aspects of both 'religious' and 'secular' violence."[142] They argue that this "is misleading" since it leads to "assumptions about the motives, causes and behaviour of groups classified as 'religious terrorist.'"[143] This is especially problematic since supposed religious terrorists are often "indistinguishable from their 'secular' counterparts."[144] As they argue, "[t]here may be a multitude of 'secular' reasons for choosing a religious target," as well as the fact that conspicuously religious attacks "may have as much to do with ethnic, political or economic motives as with religion."[145] By taking al-Qaida, "the quintessential 'religious terrorist' group," as an example, Gunning and Jackson argue that the

[141] Tomoko Masuzawa, *The Invention of World Religions: Or, how European universalism was preserved in the language of pluralism* (Chicago: University of Chicago Press, 2005); Brendt Nongbri, *Before Religion: A history of a modern concept* (New Haven and London: Yale University Press, 2013).

[142] Jeroen Gunning and Richard Jackson, "What's so 'Religious' about 'Religious Terrorism?'" *Critical Studies on Terrorism* 4(3) (2011), 370 [369–388].

[143] Gunning and Jackson, "What's," 370. [144] Gunning and Jackson, "What's," 370.

[145] Gunning and Jackson, "What's," 376.

group "displays a great many secular characteristics" regarding its strategy, choice of targets, professionalism, and pan-Islamic rhetoric.[146] Jackson considers it questionable to what degree religious markers such as rituals and notions of superhuman qualities are reserved solely for religious groups.[147]

Related to the problem of the distinction between religious and secular violence is that of Islamic terrorism, which in post-9/11 scholarship has come to signify the epitome of religious violence. As Gunning and Jackson argue, the explicatory factor of Islam as a cause of violence is at best vague. For example, while "Hamas' suicide bombing campaign and its ceasefire declarations – violent and peaceful – were justified with reference to Islam."[148] Referring to "religion" in this way is not particularly Islamic. For example, the Euskadi Ta Askatasuna (ETA), often classified as a secular-nationalist group, has been shaped by Catholicism in a fashion similar to how Islam has shaped Hamas.[149] Jackson, moreover, refers to the Chicago Project on Security and Terrorism (CPOST) to make his case. CPOST ran statistics on all suicide attacks conducted worldwide between 1982 and 2015. Jackson concludes that of the 315 cases of suicide terrorism in the database, there is no data to support a particular link between suicide terrorism and Islamic fundamentalism, or to any of the world's religions for that matter.[150] Jackson also quotes Marc Sageman's influential study of 172 members of Islamic terrorist groups,[151] which shows that

> only 17 per cent of the terrorists had an Islamic religious
> education; only 8 per cent of terrorists showed any religious

---

[146] Gunning and Jackson, "What's," 376. [147] Gunning and Jackson, "What's," 379.
[148] Gunning and Jackson, "What's," 381. [149] Gunning and Jackson, "What's," 381.
[150] CPOST in Richard Jackson, "Constructing Enemies: 'Islamic terrorism' in political and academic discourse," *Government and Opposition* 42(3) (2007), 416 [394–426].
[151] Jackson, "Constructing," 416.

devotion as youths; only 13 per cent of terrorists indicated that
they were inspired to join solely on the basis of religious beliefs;
increased religious devotion appeared to be an effect of joining
the terrorist group, not the cause of it.[152]

This leads Jackson to draw the conclusion that "Islamism is probably more
accurately described as a revolutionary ideology than a violent religious
cult."[153]

The Perennial Will to Define

Given that CTS scholars regard power and knowledge as intimately linked, that
they argue that the category terrorism has been used to serve Western powers
and to legitimize the war on terror, and that terrorism has been used to stigmatize
Islam and Muslims, "[o]ne might," as Erlenbusch states, "expect a certain
reluctance to define terrorism."[154] This is not the case. Gunning argues that "a
critically constituted field cannot afford to abandon it [the term terrorism]" for,
on the one hand, economic reasons, on the other, moral or pragmatic reasons.[155]
The economic element is important since the continuous usage of "the term
[terrorism] also increases the currency and relevance of one's research in both
funding and policy circles, as well as among the wider public."[156] To abandon the
term would, as I understand the argument, be morally wrong since the field of

[152] Jackson, "Constructing," 416.

[153] Jackson, "Constructing," 417. On this issue, also see Mark Juergensmeyer,
"Entering the Mindset of Violent Religious Activists," *Religions* 6 (2015), 852–
859.

[154] Erlenbusch, "How," 476.

[155] Jeroem Gunning, "A Case for Critical Terrorism Studies?" *Government and
Opposition* 42(3) (2007), 384 [363–393].

[156] Gunning, "A Case," 384.

terrorism studies would be up for grabs by less-educated and more ideologically biased scholars. In this vein, Jackson argues that the category is necessary to hold accountable states that support terrorism as well as to fight terrorists and their allies.[157] Also, by keeping the category, Toros and Gunning argue, critical scholars can "engage traditional scholars on their own terms, since it does not reject the category of 'terrorist violence' wholesale."[158]

How, then, is terrorism defined? According to Jackson:

> CTS views terrorism fundamentally as a strategy or tactic of political violence that can be, and frequently is, employed by both state and non-state actors and during times of war and peace … Moreover, as a strategy, terrorism involves the deliberate targeting of civilians in order to intimidate or terrorise for distinctly political purposes.[159]

Jackson et al. add that terrorism is certainly "not an ideology or a belief system."[160] "In other words" Jackson states, "terrorism is just one among several repertoires of political conflict, which also includes war, civil war, genocide, ethnic cleansing, riots, insurgency, assassination, sabotage, civil disobedience and the like."[161] Except for the incorporation of state violence, this definition is not very far from that of many mainstream scholars and, perhaps surprisingly, it even comes close to many definitions found within the mainstream field, such as the

[157] Jackson et al., *Terrorism*, 107.

[158] Harmonie Toros and Jeroen Gunning, "Exploring a Critical Theory Approach to Terrorism Studies," In Jackson et al., *Critical*, 93 [87–108].

[159] Richard Jackson, "The Core Commitments of Critical Terrorism Studies," *European Political Science* 6(3) (2007), 248 [244–251].

[160] Jackson et al., *Terrorism*, 116. [161] Jackson, "Unknown."

academic consensus definition of 1988. Jackson even states that there is actually "a general working consensus among the leading terrorism studies scholars about the core defining characteristics of terrorist violence."[162] "The real problem," according to Jackson et al., "lies in the way definitions of terrorism are typically applied in a persistently inconsistent manner by scholars in their research, and the subsequent way in which the term is frequently used as a tool of delegitimisation by political actors."[163] The mission for CTS scholars, therefore, is to invest in "a continuous process of revisiting our understandings of terrorism," which then "has the potential to prevent elites from manipulating the language of terrorism as an instrument of propaganda aimed at condemning their enemies or obscuring their own violence."[164] Ultimately, as Jackson et al. conclude, "[a]t one level, CTS can be described simply as a call for much more rigorous and sensitive research."[165]

The Emperor's New Clothes?

One of CTS's prime ambitions is to investigate "why, when, how and for what purpose do groups and individuals come to be named as 'terrorist' and what consequences does this have?"[166] But it is curious that scholars within CTS seem to forget to ask *themselves* this question, as indeed they should if core reasons to keep on using terrorism as an analytical category include getting funding and communicating with mainstream scholars, which, to a cynical mind, appears to be nothing more than an elaborate ambition to get published. Moreover, their political imperative, the use of language that frees individuals from "unnecessary structural constraints" and "avoidable human suffering," begs the question of who should

---

[162] Jackson et al., "Critical," 217. [163] Jackson et al., "Critical," 217.
[164] Jackson et al., *Terrorism*, 108. [165] Jackson et al., "Critical," 227.
[166] Jackson, "The Core," 248.

make the decision of what is "unnecessary" and "avoidable" and how that decision could ever be freed from power and ideology.

It should come as no surprise, then, that CTS scholars have been criticized, both by mainstream scholars and by more radical voices (I will return to the latter type of criticism in the final section of the Element). John Horgan and Michael Boyle, in making a case for the mainstream field, argue that CTS scholars have developed a "straw man" that in "some cases unfairly portrays almost 40 years of multi- and interdisciplinary research."[167] They argue, moreover, that CTS scholars' readings of the mainstream field are "superficial" and create "an image of the field of study unrecognizable to scholars working within it."[168] Somewhat ironically, the desire by CTS scholars to use one definition for terrorism makes Horgan and Boyle argue for plurality: "The absence of a clear, accepted definition is far from essential for conceptual development, and contrary to what CTS advocates think, the ongoing lack of definition may be a valid indicator of that very development."[169] Torsten Michel and Anthony Richards summarize the mission of CTS and argue that "a strong case has been put forward to fuse a self-reflexive engagement with mainstream assumptions about 'terrorism' with a strong normative agenda revolving around the notion of 'emancipation.'"[170] While these are important aspects for any academic field, one is left to wonder what all the, for the lack of a better word, fuzz is about. Are mainstream and critical scholars really that different or is it more a question of broadening an already existing field? Perhaps in the near future we will all talk about critical

---

[167] John Horgan and Michael J. Boyle, "A Case against 'Critical Terrorism Studies," *Critical Studies on Terrorism* 1(1) (2008), 52 [51–64].

[168] Horgan and Boyle, "A Case," 51. [169] Horgan and Boyle, "A Case," 56.

[170] Torsten Michel and Anthony Richards, "False Dawns or New Horizons? Further Issues and Challenges for Critical Terrorism Studies," *Critical Studies on Terrorism* 2 (3) (2009), 201 [399–413].

mainstream terrorism studies. Regardless, it appears as if CTS is as caught in the nexus of power and knowledge as the mainstream field. To quote Stampnitzky: "When terrorism experts level charges of politicized knowledge against each other, they are attempting to manage both the field of expertise and the proper definition of terrorism itself."[171] There is also more to it than the definition of terrorism. It appears as if the whole analytical project both questions commonsensical usages of central categories such as religion, violence, and politics and continues to use them in the commonsensical way that they critique. As Erlenbusch astutely states: "Not only does this view reproduce key elements of many mainstream definitions of terrorism, but also it belies the alleged anti-naturalism, anti-essentialism, and anti-determinism of CTS by having to determine the specific difference that distinguishes the tactic of terrorism from other forms of political violence."[172]

European Jihad(ism)

Since the 1980s, member states of the EU have been the arena for a number of plots and attacks by perpetrators usually categorized as "Islamic terrorists" or "jihadists": the murder of Theo van Gogh in Amsterdam in 2004; the train station bombings in Madrid in 2004, killing 191 and injuring around 1,800; the underground and bus bombings in London in 2005, claiming more than 50 victims; the attack against the satirical magazine *Charlie Hebdo* and the following attack against the Jewish supermarket Hyper Cacher in Paris, killing 17 and injuring two dozen; the synchronized attack in the concert hall Bataclan, the football stadium Stade de France, and several restaurants in central Paris in 2015, killing 130 and injuring nearly 400; and the synchronized attacks in

---

[171] Stampnitzky, *Disciplining*, 8. [172] Erlenbusch, "How," 476.

Brussels 2016, claiming at least 35 deaths and injuring more than 200.[173] This is far from a complete list of the attacks classified as "Islamic terrorist," but they are the most sensational and mediatized.[174] What made these cases even more noteworthy was that they were classified as "homegrown," "self-recruited," and "self-radicalized," that is, committed by European nationals.[175]

Much has been written about the perpetrators of the attacks and their motives. The fact that many of the perpetrators died during or after the attacks does not help in the quest for answers, since, to paraphrase Talal Asad, trying to understand them becomes a matter of retroactively ascribing meaning to their acts.[176] This is, of course, not a problem exclusive to terrorism studies. Research in the humanities and social sciences is generally a matter of retroactively ascribing meaning to events. However, what makes the field particularly difficult are the political factors involved, including the immediacy of the events, the call to vengeance by outside voices such as politicians and the news media, and the self-policing moralizing of the field itself. Drawing the line between understanding and legitimizing terrorism has been a topic for much debate.[177]

---

[173] For detailed accounts of these attacks, see Petter Nesser, *Islamist Terrorism in Europe: A history* (London: Hurst & Company, 2016).

[174] For a comprehensive account, see Petter Nesser, "Jihadism in Western Europe After the Invasion of Iraq: Tracing motivational influences from the Iraq War on jihadist terrorism in Western Europe," *Studies in Conflict & Terrorism* 29(4) (2006), 323–342; Petter Nesser, "Chronology of Jihadism in Western Europe 1994–2007: Planned, prepared, and executed terrorist attacks," *Studies in Conflict & Terrorism*, 31(10) (2008), 924–946; Petter Nesser, "Toward an Increasingly Heterogeneous Threat: A chronology of jihadist terrorism in Europe 2008–2013," *Studies in Conflict & Terrorism* 37(5) (2014), 440–456.

[175] See Manni Crone and Martin Harrow, "Homegrown Terrorism in the West," *Terrorism and Political Violence* 23(4) (2011), 521–536.

[176] Talal Asad, *On Suicide Bombing* (New York: Columbia University Press, 2007), 45.

[177] On the issue of moralizing and taboos, see Nesser, "Chronology," 925; Nilsson, "Where's"; Joseba Zulaika, "Drones, Witches and Other Flying Objects: The force of fantasy in US counterterrorism," *Critical Studies on Terrorism* 5(1) (2012), 51–68.

These aspects aside, another problem is that the perpetrators have been rather sparing in leaving traces for the afterworld to study. Moreover, since the traces that do exist often end up in the hands of national security services, they are beyond the reach of the general scholar. This means that scholars are often forced to search for small pieces to complete the terrorism puzzle. As Peter Nesser states, "[w]ith no single document specifying the causes, aims, and strategic visions of militants in Europe, there is a need to rely on other indicators."[178] As stated in the previous sections, the lack of firsthand sources seems endemic to the whole field. For example, when Nesser paints the picture of Islamist terrorism in Europe, the sources mentioned are the media, interviews with experts, judicial papers, and a jihadi primary source. However, while the predicaments involved by relying on the three first sources are discussed, the only primary source (jihadi material) is left out, meaning that the reader is left to assume that this data is collected from the media.[179]

Given the known difficulties obtaining primary material to explain why these attacks happened, the entrance at the beginning of the twenty-first century of the theory of radicalization in the academic arena provided an ontological and epistemological framework that could bring all the puzzle pieces together.[180] In understanding terrorism, radicalization was perceived as a more balanced account than Bernard Lewis and Samuel Huntington's clash of civilization thesis or the Bush administration's division of the world

---

[178] Petter Nesser, "Ideologies of Jihad in Europe," *Terrorism and Political Violence* 23 (2) (2011), 173–200.

[179] Nesser, *Islamic*, 19.

[180] See Mohammed Hafez and Creighton Mullins, "The Radicalization Puzzle: A theoretical synthesis of empirical approaches to homegrown extremism," *Studies in Conflict & Terrorism* 38(11) (2015), 958–975.

into good and evil.[181] Indeed, radicalization has today become one of the most important tropes in the discourse of Islamic terrorism and is held as the explicatory model for "what goes on before the bomb goes off."[182] The trope refers to the various ways in which a normal male Muslim, having passed through one of the many sites of radicalization, be it the "online university" or the prison yard, chooses to strap a bomb belt around his chest to blow himself up while declaring takbir,[183] with the aim of bringing as much death and destruction with him as possible.[184] Radicalization has become such a potent trope that it is used as a self-explicatory category by academics, politicians, and journalists to explain the reasons for attacks on civilians on European soil by creating an imagined and often imprecise image of groups of

[181] Arun Kundnani, "Radicalisation: The journey of a concept," *Race & Class* 54(2) (2009), 5 [3–25].

[182] Mark Sedgwick, "The Concept of Radicalization as a Source of Confusion," *Terrorism and Political Violence* 22(4) (2010), 479 [479–494].

[183] Takbir ...

[184] On sites of radicalization, see Evan F. Kohlmann, "'Homegrown' Terrorists: Theory and cases in the war on terror's newest front," *The Annals of the American Academy of Political and Social Science* 618 (2008), 97–98 [95–109]; Farhad Khosrokhavar, "Radicalization in Prison: The French case," *Politics, Religion & Ideology* 14(2) (2013), 284–306; Anne Stenersen"The Internet: A virtual training camp?" *Terrorism and Political Violence*, 20(2) (2008), 215–233; Gabriel Weimann, *Terror on the Internet: The new arena, the new challenges* (Washington, DC: United States Institute of Peace Press, 2006), 123–129. On masculinity and war, see Zillah Eisenstein, "Resexing Militarism for the Globe," in *Feminism and War: Confronting US imperialism*, eds. Robin L. Riley, Chandra Talpade Mohany, and Minnie Bruce Pratt (London and New York: Zed Books, 2008), 27–46; Joane Nagel, "Masculinity and Nationalism: Gender and sexuality in the making of nations," *Ethnic and Racial Studies* 21(2) (2010), 242–269. On terrorism and gender, see Karla J. Cunningham, "Cross-Regional Trends in Female Terrorism," *Studies in Conflict & Terrorism*, 26 (3) (2003), 171–195.

Muslim youth as the "enemy within."[185] Like the category of Islamic terrorism, the category of radicalization is not neutral or objective. With it follows a contingent history, dubious truth claims, and an explicatory model that has been criticized for doing more harm than good. In mainstream approaches to radicalization, the theory of new terrorism has been baked into its ontological and epistemological foundation. As Arun Kundnani explains: "An a priori distinction is drawn between the new terrorism, seen as originating in Islamist theology, and the old terrorism of nationalist or Leftist political violence, for which the question of radicalization is rarely posed."[186]

In this section, I set out to map the ontology and epistemology of the trope of radicalization in mainstream and critical terrorism studies. The section is structured around a common way of describing radicalization. First of all, this means describing the supposed ideology lurking behind it – "Salafism" or "Salafi-Jihadism." Second, I sketch the contours of radicalization as a process of recruitment, whereby an individual comes to take on an acclaimed Salafist or Salafi-Jihadist world view. In this section, I also discuss more specifically the category of radicalization and its different and contested meanings.

The Ideology Behind

In the quest for pieces to complete the radicalization puzzle, scholars have recently paid the ideology driving the process a great deal of attention. The academic interest in Islam, Muslims, and violence has a long history in Europe, but it was not until the 1980s that Islamic fundamentalism became a proper topic

[185] Orla Lynch, "British Muslim Youth: Radicalisation, terrorism and the construction of the 'other,'" *Critical Studies on Terrorism*, 6(2) (2013), 243 [241–261].

[186] Kundnani, *The Muslims*, 208.

of enquiry.[187] While Islamic fundamentalism soon became a reoccurring topic in academia, in the political arena and in the news media, it was juxtaposed to, and by more well-read experts replaced with, the category "Salafism." As Roel Meijer notes, Salafism did not attract much attention before 9/11, except for a few scholars (e.g., Gilles Kepel and Reinhard Schulze), but this changed with the emerging theory of radicalization.[188] Lately, Salafism has also come to be further explained through the category of "Jihadism." Jarret Brachman states: "Jihadism cannot be extricated from the religious and ideological context from which it emerged: Salafism."[189] What does the literature tell us about these categories and their role in the discourse of Islamic terrorism?

Salafism

Quintan Wiktorowicz explains that Salafists[190] "are united by a common religious creed" that "revolves around strict adherence to the concept of tawhid (the oneness of God) and ardent rejection of a role for human reason, logic, and desire."[191] He continues:

---

[187] E.g., Bernard Lewis, *The Crisis of Islam: Holy war and unholy terror* (London: Pheonix, 2005). For critical research on the topic, see Tomaz Mastnak, *Crusading Peace: Christendom, the Muslim world, and Western political order* (Berkeley: University of California Press, 2002); Masuzawa, The Invention.

[188] Roel Meijer, "Introduction," in *Global Salafism: Islam's new religious movement*, ed. Roel Meijer (New York: Oxford University Press, 2013), 1–2 [1–32].

[189] Jarret M. Brachman, *Global Jihadism: Theory and practice* (London and New York: Routledge, 2009), 23.

[190] Salafi(s) and Salafist(s) are used interchangeably throughout the literature. Wiktorowicz uses the former; I will henceforth use the latter.

[191] Quintan Wiktorowicz, "Anatomy of the Salafi Movement," *Studies in Conflict & Terrorism* 29 (2006), 207 [207–239].

> Salafis believe that by strictly following the rules and guidance in the Qur'an and Sunna (path or example of the Prophet Muhammad) they eliminate the biases of human subjectivity and self-interest, thereby allowing them to identify the singular truth of God's commands. From this perspective, there is only one legitimate religious interpretation; Islamic pluralism does not exist.[192]

Salafists may share a common creed but, Wiktorowicz points out, "divisions have emerged as a result of the inherently subjective nature of applying religion to new issues and problems," meaning that, although Salafists "share the same approach to religious jurisprudence, they often hold different interpretations about contemporary politics and conditions."[193]

Salafism is indeed a category with many meanings. Thomas Hegghammer notes that outside observers tend to use the category as a descriptive one, while those self-identifying as Salafists use it normatively.[194] Regardless, it is used as a classificatory and descriptive category within terrorism studies. Juan Carlos Antúnez and Ioannis Tellidis argue that Salafism emerged during the nineteenth century as a "modernist, intellectual movement" with a puritan but non-authoritarian approach to the Islamic sources.[195] Their goal was to bridge the technological and civilizational gaps between the West and the Islamic world. However, they say, "politics is not Salafism's ultimate objective."[196] Instead, it is to educate

---

[192] Wiktorowicz, "Anatomy," 207. [193] Wiktorowicz, "Anatomy," 208.

[194] Thomas Hegghammer, "Jihadi-Salafis or Revolutionaries? On Religion and Politics in the Study of Militant Islamism," in Meijer, "Introduction," 248 [244–280].

[195] Juan Carlos Antúnez and Ioannis Tellidis, "The Power of Words: The deficient terminology surrounding Islam-related terrorism," *Critical Studies on Terrorism* 6(1) (2013), 126 [118–139].

[196] Antúnez and Tellidis, "The Power," 126.

Muslims about what according to Salafists are their true Islamic duties. Drawing on Wiktorowiz, they argue that Salafism ought to be divided into three sub-groups: "purists, politicos and jihadis."[197] They moreover deplore journalists' sloppy usage of the category that often brings with it connotations of terrorism. Journalists rarely delve into the "nuances" and confuse the different Salafi subgroups with one another. To remedy this problem, they argue that any usage of the category "should be preceded by a more careful and prudent examination" and "particularly by the media."[198]

Now, this is a curious claim since the authors themselves talk about Salafism as one ideology, as one *-ism*, and, moreover, that out of the examples of the modern split within Salafism, purists, politicos, and jihadis, only one seems to fit their generalization that the purists are the only ones not political or violent. Moreover, the division of Salafists into three groups seems imprecise if compared to writings of certain self-avowed Salafists themselves. Jarret Brachman, who provides one of the most detailed accounts of Salafism within the field of terrorism studies,[199] makes this point by referring to the writings of Dr. Tariq Abdelhaleem, who divides Salafism into no less than eight subgroups: "'Establishment Salafists,' 'Madkhali (or Jami) Salafists,' 'Albani Salafists,' 'Scientific Salafists,' 'Salafist Ikhwan (Muslim Brotherhood),' 'Sururis,' 'Qutubis,' and 'Global Jihadists.'"[200] It is the last that is of concern here.

---

[197] Antúnez and Tellidis, "The Power," 126.

[198] Antúnez and Tellidis, "The Power," 128.

[199] For more detailed accounts on Salafism, see Michael Cook, *Commanding Right and Forbidding Wrong in Islamic Thought* (Cambridge: Cambridge University Press, 2006); Richard Gauvain, *Salafi Ritual Purity: In the presence of God* (London and New York: Routledge, 2013); Meijer, *Global*; Joas Wagemaker, "The Enduring Legacy of the Second Saudi State: Quietist and radical Wahhabi contestations of *al-walā' wa al-barā'*," *International Journal of Middle Eastern Studies* 44(1) (2012), 93–110.

[200] Brachman, *Global*, 26.

The global jihadists movement began, Brachman states, "as nothing more than a distillation of the most conservative and violent tendencies from the other seven categories of Salafism."[201] The ideologues cultivating these tendencies have roots in Saudi Arabia from the 1970s, most notably with Adbullah Yusuf Azzam, Usama Bin Ladin's mentor, co-founder of al-Qaida, and the infamous "Father of Global Jihad" or "Emir of Jihad." Azzam's motto was "Jihad and the rifle alone: no negotiations, no conferences, and no dialogues."[202] While iconic figures in the ideology include the world-renowned Bin Laden, Abu Musab al-Zarqawi, and Ayman al-Zawahiri, there exist a plethora of global jihadist thinkers. For example, Abu Qatada al-Filistini, Abd al-Qadir ibn abd al-Aziz, Abu Muhammad al-Maqdisi, and Nasr Bin al-Fahd have by "tapping into existing religious concepts, histories and beliefs ... had enormous success building their version of God's army on Earth."[203] While their conspicuously religious language might seem archaic, the logic behind it, argues Frazer Egerton, is rather unexceptional: "Militant leftists materialise from the trade union movements and workers' parties, animal rights militants from animal welfare advocates and environmental campaigners. Militant Salafism is unexceptional in following the same political rule."[204]

Jihadism

What about jihadism as ideology? Brachman summarizes seven "interlocking elements" of the Global Jihadist ideology, which he also simply refers to as "Jihadism." First of all, the ideology is constructed on a founding myth, wherein the Prophet Muhammed and his nearest followers are made into the

---

[201] Brachman, *Global*, 26.

[202] John L. Esposito, *Unholy War: Terror in the name of Islam* (Oxford: Oxford University Press, 2002), 7ff.

[203] Brachman, *Global*, 11.

[204] Frazer Egerton, *Jihad in the West: The rise of militant Salafism* (Cambridge: Cambridge University Press, 2011), 133.

perfect examples to mimic. For this purpose, puritan medieval Islamic literature as well as publications from modern Salafist thinkers comprise the source material. Second, the ideology's core principles are tawhid (the oneness and totality of God), al-wala' wa-l-bara' (loyalty to God, Islam, and Muslims and disloyalty to non-Muslims), jihad (struggle or war), aqida (the Islamic creed), and takfir (declaration of apostates). They have been declared and described by ideologues such as Muhammad Ibn abd al-Wahab, Hasan al-Banna, Sayyid Qutb, Maududi, Juhayman al-Utaybi, among others. The third element concerns the practical application of these principles by leaders including Marwan Hadid, Abdullah Azzam, Mullah Muhammad Umar, Bin Laden, al-Zawahiri, Khattab, Yusuf al-Ayiri, and al-Zarqawi. Fourth, "ideological guidance" is provided by intellectuals such as Hammoud bin Uqla as-Shuaybi, Abu Muhamamd al-Maqdisi, Nasr al-Fahd, Ali al-Khudayr, Abu Qatada, Abu Basir al-Tartusi, Umar Abd al-Rahman, and many more. Fifth, the ideology is reproduced through the "ever-expanding accessibility of information and education made possible by jihadist propaganda groups, such as as-Sahab, al-Furqan, Sawt al-Jihad, al-Fajr, Global Islamic Media Front, and others." Sixth, strategists including Abu Ubayd al-Qurashi, Abu Musab al-Suri, Abu Bakr Naji, and Lewis Atiyattallah provide strategic guidance. The final element is the increasing grassroots movement of (future) Salafists based on "study groups, internet forums and self-guided Jihadist curricula."[205]

Of the core principles, jihad is by far the most (in)famous. Jihad has been widely discussed by both mainstream and critical terrorism scholars.[206] Jihad is,

---

[205] Brachman, *Global*, 41.

[206] E.g., Deina Abdelkader, "Coercion, Peace and the Issue of Jihad," *Digest of Middle East Studies* 20(2) (2011), 178–185; James L. Gelvin, "Nationalism, Anarchism, Reform: Political Islam from the inside out," *Middle East Policy* 13(3) (2010), 118–133; Rudolph Peters, *Jihad in Classical and Modern Islam: A reader* (Princeton: Markus Wiener Publications, 1996).

as Shireen Khan Burki says, "a widely (mis)interpreted concept"[207] and, in Western media, as Antúnez and Tellidis point out, commonly described as meaning "Holy War."[208] But anyone looking for a universal definition will be disappointed. John Eposito, who gives a general answer to the question of what jihad is, manages to deduce three widely disparate meanings for the category:

> One might say that jihad is striving to lead a good Muslim life, praying and fasting regularly, being an attentive spouse and parent. Another might identify jihad as working hard to spread the message of Islam. For a third, it might be supporting the struggle of oppressed Muslim peoples in Palestine, Kashmir, Chechnya, or Kosovo. And for the final speaker, as for Osama bin Laden, jihad could mean working to overthrow governments in the Muslim world and attacking America. However different these interpretations are, all testify to the centrality of jihad for Muslims today. Jihad is a defining concept or belief in Islam, a key element in what it means to be a believer and follower of God's Will.[209]

Waging jihad on a daily basis by living a faithful life and being a good parent is, of course, quite different from embarking on war against the world's largest military power. Further distinctions can be made in jihad as warfare: offensive and defensive warfare. However, this is no different from premodern legal and ideological systems that developed equivalents of today's "just warfare"

---

[207] Shireen Khan Burki, "Haram or Halal? Islamists' Use of suicide attacks as 'Jihad,'" *Terrorism and Political Violence* 23(4) (2011), 582 [582–601].

[208] Antúnez and Tellidis, "The Power," 129. [209] Esposito, *Unholy*, 26.

theories.[210] As Nelly Lahoud points out, offensive warfare has been strictly regulated in Islamic legal doctrine, while the defensive has not.[211] Lahoud, moreover, points out, "Jihadis all agree that this doctrine of defensive jihad defines their rationale for embracing jihad" and adds, "jihadis have plausibly adapted defensive jihad to argue that their actions are justified and lawful."[212] Waging a global jihad is thus legitimized by the understanding that Islam is under global attack. Jihadist ideology describes a global conspiracy with the goal of removing Islam from the face of the earth. The conspiracy is supposedly led by Christian liberal democracies; the Crusaders; and their foremost allies, the Jewish Zionists; as well as Shia Muslims who try to undermine Islam from within.[213] Brachman states that this grievance was popularized by Bin Laden and al-Qaida, exemplified by Bin Laden's famous statement from 1996:

> It should not be hidden from you that the people of Islam had suffered from aggression, iniquity and injustice imposed on them by the Zionist–Crusaders alliance and their collaborators; to the extent that the Muslims' blood became the cheapest and their wealth as loot in the hands of the enemies.[214]

This victimization is, according to Bachman, "the backbone of a global jihadist movement."[215]

[210] On premodern just war, Gregory M. Reichberg, Henrik Syse, and Endre Begby, *The Ethics of War: Classic and contemporary readings* (Oxford: Blackwell Publishing, 2006).

[211] Nelly Lahoud, "The Neglected Sex: The jihadis' exclusion of women from jihad," *Terrorism and Political Violence* 26(5) (2014), 780–802.

[212] Lahoud, "The Neglected," 783. [213] Brachman, *The Global*, 11.

[214] Brachman, *The Global*, 11. [215] Brachman, *The Global*, 11.

Critical and mainstream scholars may debate the historical, juridical, and theological foundations of jihadism or militant Salafism, but a larger consensus on the ideological base seems to exist. However, when it comes to the legitimacy of these claims, scholars are more divided. Few scholars actually seem to take the words of the jihadi ideologues seriously. The moralizing imperative of the field makes itself felt – where are scholars to draw the line between understanding terrorism and potentially legitimizing it? The stakes are high and the conclusions drawn from critical analysis would, if they were made into political policy, have far-reaching consequences. For example, Michael Mann has compellingly argued against the theory of new terrorism and the advocates of the clash of civilization thesis. Mann states that Bin Ladin was not aiming at waging a war against the Western way of life: "He barely said a word about Western culture. He did not denounce materialism or consumerism or Christian dogma or liberated women."[216] Bin Laden was concerned with imperialism "brutally seizing land and property by force of arms" and, as a "rational man," there is "a simple *reason* why he attacked the US: American imperialism," and, "as long as America seeks to control the Middle East, he and people like him will be its enemy."[217] The continued US interventions in the Middle East and the rise of the Islamic State seem to confirm Mann's thesis.[218]

---

[216] Michael Mann, *Incoherent Empire* (London: Verso, 2003), 169.

[217] Mann, *Incoherent*, 169. Also see Peter L. Bergen, *Holy War Inc.: Inside the secret world of Osama Bin Ladin* (London: Phoenix, 2001).

[218] For literature on ISIS, see Abdel Bari Atwan, *Islamic State: The digital caliphate* (London: Saqi Books, 2015); Jean-Pierre Filiu, *From Deep State to Islamic State: The Arab counter-revolution and its jihadi legacy* (London: Hurs & Company, 2015); Pierre-Jean Luizar, *Le piège Daech: L'État Islamique ou le retour de l'Histoire* (Paris: La Découverte, 2015); Loretta Napoleoni, *The Islamist Phoenix: The Islamic State (ISIS) and the redrawing of the Middle East* (New York: Open Stories, 2014).

The recent years also have seen a change in the jihadism ideology. Nesser points out that although al-Zawahiri regards Syria as the most important area in which to practice jihad, he states that "all Mujahid brothers must consider targeting the interests of the western Zionist-Crusader alliance in any part of the world as their foremost duty."[219] This call is in line with the aforementioned idea of open source jihad, as presented as a strategy by AQIP in its e-magazine *Inspire* and ISIS's *Dabiq*.[220] One interesting aspect of these magazines is that many of the jihadi strategies described call into question the theory of terrorism as communication. Several articles in *Inspire*, for example, call for what Sarah Marsden et al. refer to as "popular resistance," which implies destroying buildings, causing traffic accidents, torching parked cars, causing forest fires, and other techniques. What they have in common is that they are supposed to "look like an accident."[221] If they indeed look like an accident, then there is no explanation to be found, thus no sender or receiver of any messages. This points to a larger problem of definition. Christina Hellmich points out that although Salafism and Whahabbism are commonsensically taken as the ideological underpinnings of al-Qaida, exactly how and what are being brought into the jihadist ideology, except from the "occasional citations from fatwas and recent video messages" from the classical ideologues is unclear: "we are told

---

[219] Petter Nesser, "Toward an Increasingly Heterogeneous Threat: A chronology of jihadist terrorism in Europe 2008–2013," *Studies in Conflict & Terrorism* 37(5) (2014), 440 [440–456].

[220] See Anthony F. Lemieux, Jarret M. Brachman, Jason Levitt, and Jay Wood, "Inspire Magazine: A critical analysis of its significance and potential impact through the lens of the information, motivation, and behavioral skills model," *Terrorism and Political Violence* 26(2) (2014), 356 [354–371].

[221] Sarah Marsden, Daiana Marino, and Gilbert Ramsay, "Forest Jihad: Assessing the evidence for 'popular resistance terrorism,'" *Studies in Conflict & Terrorism* 37(1) (2014), 2 [1–17].

very little about where, when, and how bin Laden, or al-Zawahiri for that matter, draw from these various sources."[222] Given the many variants of Salafism and their inner contradictions, is it possible to even talk about Salafism as the underpinning of jihadism? And is jihadism a valid category? "In other words," as Hellmich states, "the 'Salafi-jihadist' discourse that seems to have become the underlying ideology of Al Qaeda lacks a definitional basis and remains vague at best. As such, it does not seem to be particularly rewarding to use this discourse as a means to explaining the logic that underlies Al Qaeda."[223]

If it is hard to pinpoint in exactly what way Salafism makes the ideological base for al-Qaida; it seems even more difficult to discern how Salafism relates to "Islamic terrorism" in Europe. As Egerton points out, a number of scholars have "explored the idea of the political imaginary in the context of militant Salafism, including some of the finest scholars in the area."[224] Many scholars in the field of terrorism studies as well as Islamic studies seem to agree on the point that Salafism holds a certain appeal for marginalized young Muslims in Europe. Meijer concludes that in a "contentious age," Salafism serves the "humiliated, the downtrodden, disgruntled young people, the discriminated migrant, or the politically repressed" and offers them membership of "a chosen sect" with "direct access to the truth."[225] Mohamed-Ali Adraoui makes a similar argument by stating that Salafism provides "dropouts" a "transcendental dimension, a holy identity, and the belief that they are chosen."[226] Adraoui adds: "Where before the migrant lived on the fringe of society (mentally rather than

---

[222] Hellmich, "Creating," 120. [223] Hellmich, "Creating," 119.

[224] Egerton, *Jihad*, 54. [225] Meijer, "Introduction," 13.

[226] Mohamed-Ali Adraoui, "Salafism in France: Ideology, practices and contradictions," in *Global Salafism: Islam's new religious movement*, ed. Roel Meijer (New York: Oxford University Press, 2013), 367 [364–383].

effectively), as a Salafi he now stands at the centre of the world and embodies a sacred history."[227] However, why Salafists would also be prone to violence is not explained. This is where theories of radicalization come into play.

Radicalization

The category of radicalization is a relative newcomer in the discourse on Islamic terrorism.[228] As Mark Sedgwick notes, the category was quasi-absent in Western news media before 9/11. In academia, however, it was used by a few; Olivier Roy, for example, included radicalization in his writings during the early 1990s. The category certainly had a meaning similar to that of today, and Roy talks about the "political radicalization of the entire Muslim world," referring to the tense political situations of the 1960s.[229] Roy calls the Rushdie affair "a good example of this radicalization of popular Islam."[230] However, it is not described as a process or path leading to terrorism, as is the case today.

The Category Emerges

In Europe, the category makes its grand entrance in academia, the political arena, and the news media in 2004–2005.[231] The category quickly turns into an explicative moment for the linkage between the violent Islamic world over

---

[227] Adraoui, "Salafism," 367.

[228] For a more extensive overview, see Anja Dalgaard-Nielsen, "Violent Radicalization in Europe: What we know and what we do not know," *Studies in Conflict & Terrorism* 33(9) (2010), 797–814; Alex P. Schmid, "Radicalisiation, De-Radicalisation, Counter-Radicalisation: A conceptual discussion and literature review," *ICCT Research Paper* March (2013), 1 [online].

[229] Olivier Roy, *The Failure of Political Islam* (Cambridge: Cambridge University Press, 1994), 77.

[230] Roy, *The Failure*, 88. [231] Sedgwick, *The Concept*, 480.

"there" and the democratic peaceful world "here."[232] Before the category of radicalization, scholars had certainly debated what brings individuals and groups to commit violent acts, as discussed in the previous section. A long-standing debate has been whether a bottom-up or a top-down perspective is more accurate in describing this transition to violence.[233] Related to this debate is the one on the motives behind suicide attacks. Pape and Feldman conclude that before 9/11, "the expert debate on the causes of suicide terrorism was divided largely between two explanations: religious fanaticism and mental illness."[234] The idea of a specific Muslim psyche, extra prone to violence, became in certain circles an unquestioned truth where, as Hellmich has put it, "[t]errorism at the hands of Islamists is thereby symbolically transformed into the terminal stage of a general Muslim malady."[235] One proponent of this view was Laurent Murawiec, who claimed that "the idea of murdering, maiming, and menacing the enemy for the purpose of hastening the final triumph of Islam has always held a very strong appeal among the Muslim masses"[236] and, moreover, "there is no firewall between Mahdism and mainstream Islam, since it is all 'in the Book.'"[237] To paraphrase Hellmich, theories of this sort not only denigrate Muslims in general; they also draw on colonial narratives of the native culture as sick and in need of Western civilization as a cure.[238] Today, however, the theory of the mentally ill jihadi has less bearing, although

[232] Kundnani, *The Muslims.*

[233] E.g., Walter Reich, ed., *Origins of Terrorism: Psychologies, ideologies, theologies, states of mind* (Washington: The Woodrow Wilson Center Press, 1998).

[234] Pape and Feldman, *Cutting*, 8. [235] Hellmich, "Creating," 113.

[236] Laurent Murawiec, *The Mind of Jihad* (Cambridge: Cambridge University Press, 2008), 48.

[237] Murawiec, *The Mind*, 325. [238] Hellmich, "Creating," 113.

scholars still seek answers to the imagined "Jihadi mind."[239] In their study of suicide bombers, Pape and Feldman argue that while "many were religious ... virtually none could be diagnosed as mentally ill."[240] This does not mean that psychology has been abandoned in the quest for puzzle pieces, rather that it is viewed as one factor among many.[241]

Part of laying out the puzzle of radicalization is to define its overarching meaning, but, so far, there is no academic consensus about definitions of the kind made about terrorism. Schmid even calls the quest to define radicalization a "frustrating experience" and that radicalization and other central categories (e.g., terrorism and extremism) "still present an obstacle that needs to be overcome."[242] Rick Coolsaet similarly states that "the more research produced on the issue of radicalisation, the clearer it became that the very notion of radicalisation was ill-defined, complex and controversial."[243] Notwithstanding, as Michael King and Donald Taylor state, "radicalization in its current form is most often used to describe a phenomenon that leads to homegrown terrorism," because, according to the authors, "an increasing number of terrorist acts in Western countries have been attributed to local groups, often unconnected to Al Qaeda, but very much inspired by Al Qaeda."[244] As they say, just as the meaning of a terrorist has changed, so has the meaning of radicalization:

---

[239] For an overview, see Stéphane J. Baele, "Are Terrorists 'Insane'"? A Critical Analysis of Mental Health Categories in Lone Terrorists' Trials," *Critical Studies on Terrorism* 7(2) (2014), 257–276.

[240] Pape and Feldman, *Cutting*, 8.

[241] Hafez and Creighton, "The Radicalization," 959. [242] Schmid, "Radicalisiation," 1.

[243] Rick Coolsaet, ed., *Jihadi Terrorism and the Radicalisation Challenge: European and American experiences* (Farnham: Ashgate, 2011), 240.

[244] Michael King and Donald M. Taylor, "The Radicalization of Homegrown Jihadists: A review of theoretical models and social psychological evidence," *Terrorism and Political Violence* 23(4) (2011), 603 [602–622].

"Initially a terrorist group was conceived as individuals who were foreign born, foreign trained, and covertly entering a Western country."[245] Although they leave out a large part of the genealogy of the category "terrorist," they capture how the element of the "homegrown" has become a game changer in the discourse on Islamic terrorism. Angel Rabasa and Cheryl Benard ponder the question of "homegrown" terrorists who have committed attacks in Europe. On the surface, they all appeared "to be well integrated" since they "spoke their new home countries' language – Spanish, English, or Dutch," which, considering that "they were born and educated in European countries," might appear as no surprise.[246]

Passage à l'act

Now, even if radicalization is a contested concept, there appears to be a consensus to view it as the *passage à l'act* of the "homegrown" terrorist. From here, though, a wide variety of models of radicalization, explication of root causes, and typologies of individuals prone to radicalization follow. It is common in the literature to refer to the so-called Sageman vs. Hoffman debate. Sageman is the advocate of a leader-less, bottom-up perspective, and Hoffman, who actually rarely explicitly uses the category of radicalization, is the advocate

of a leader-led, top-down perspective.[247] According to Kundnani, Sageman's writings are "perhaps the most ambitious attempt to develop a comprehensive

---

[245] King and Taylor, "The Radicalization," 604.

[246] Angel Rabasa and Cheryl Benard, *Eurojihad: Patterns of Islamist radicalization and terrorism in Europe* (New York: Cambridge University Press, 2015).

[247] See Nesser, *Islamist*, 3ff; Manni Crone and Martin Harrow, "Homegrown Terrorism in the West," *Terrorism and Political Violence*, 23(4) (2011), 521–536.

theory of radicalization."[248] Sageman, who declares that he "talks with Muslims," argues as follows:

> Contrary to popular belief, radicalization into terrorism is not the product of poverty, various forms of brain-washing, youth, ignorance or lack of education, lack of employment, lack of social responsibility, criminality, or mental illness. The mobilization of young people into this violent social movement is based on friendship and kinship.[249]

Terrorists are, according to Sageman, "simply young people seeking fame and thrills, like all the terrorists all over the world in the past 130 years."[250] They are "enthusiastic volunteers, trying to impress their friends with their heroism and sacrifice … chasing dreams of glory by fighting for justice and fairness as they define it," and they have "become the rock stars of young Muslim militants."[251] Similar to Salafists, they "believe that they are special, part of a small vanguard trying to build a better world" that is "modeled on the community around the Prophet because they claim that it was the only time in world history when a just and fair community existed."[252] For this utopia, they "are willing to sacrifice themselves … in the name of God."[253]

These future militant rock stars do not just suddenly end up sacrificing themselves for God but have gone through a process consisting of four factors: "a sense of moral outrage, a specific interpretation of the world, resonance with

[248] Kundnani, *The Muslims*, 225.

[249] Marc Sageman, "A Strategy for Fighting International Islamist Terrorists," *Annals of the American Academy of Political and Social Science* 618(1) (2008), 225.

[250] Sageman, "A Strategy," 224.   [251] Sageman, "A Strategy," 225.

[252] Sageman, "A Strategy," 224.   [253] Sageman, "A Strategy," 224.

personal experiences, and mobilization through networks."[254] Sageman stresses that this is not a matter of "stages in a process, nor do they occur sequentially; they are simply four recurrent phases in this process."[255] Among the Muslims Sageman has "talked to," one recurrent theme is "a sense of outrage" against "global and local moral violations" against Muslims, which are interpreted as "examples of a unified Western global strategy, namely, a war against Islam."[256] The emotional aspect of the moral outrage is important since, as Sageman suggests, "experts have focused far too much on ideology."[257] Instead, Sageman says:

> The explanation for their behavior is not found in how they think, but rather in how they feel. All these perpetrators dream about becoming Islamic heroes in this war against Islam, modeling themselves on the seventh-century warriors who conquered half the world and on the mujahedin who defeated the Soviet Union in Afghanistan in the 1980s. Many hope to emulate their predecessors now by fighting in Iraq against coalition forces.[258]

Why Sageman finds it necessary to separate emotions, dreams, and warrior ideals from ideology is given no further explanation, nor how ideology is defined for that matter. He also argues that the factor of personal experience is related to these young Muslims' integration, or lack thereof. Sageman argues that in Europe, "the myth of a national essence excludes non-European immigrants," which leads "Muslims [to] complain about discrimination in the labor market."[259] This is expressed as a paradoxical or ironic situation since, as Sageman suggests, "[i]n essence, European nations contribute to the funding of

---

[254] Sageman, "A Strategy," 225. [255] Sageman, "A Strategy," 225.
[256] Sageman, "A Strategy," 225. [257] Sageman, "A Strategy," 226.
[258] Sageman, "A Strategy," 226. [259] Sageman, "A Strategy," 226.

terrorist operations through welfare payments, allowing young Muslims to seek the thrill of participating in clandestine operations to escape the boredom of idleness."[260] Sageman concludes: "These factors, taken together, influence some young Muslims to become angry; network mobilization allows a very small number of them to become terrorists."[261]

Hoffman, like many scholars within the field, is explicit not only in how his work should be the basis for counterterrorism policies but also in his criticism of Sageman: "Marc Sageman claims that al Qaeda's leadership is finished and today's terrorist threat comes primarily from below. But the terrorist elites are alive and well, and ignoring the threat they pose will have disastrous consequences."[262] Hoffman, moreover, attacks Sageman's methodology: "From a social science perspective, however, these types of unidentified or vaguely identified data sources and unclear collection procedures pose serious problems."[263] While Hoffman concurs with Sageman that radicalization is real, he argues that "Sageman fails to see that the current threat is not only the product of radicalization but also the realization of strategic organizational decisions al Qaeda made at least a decade ago."[264] Hoffman's approach appears less an outright rejection of Sageman's than bringing attention to the top-down, or leader-led, aspect of radicalization.

Commenting on radicalization in "Muslim diasporas" in Europe, Hoffman identifies three types of potential terrorists. The first type is "converts to Islam," who are divided into "'hardcore,' long-term jihadis trained in camps" and "'walk-ins,' self-radicalized individuals who join the jihadist

[260] Sageman, "A Strategy," 226–227. [261] Sageman, "A Strategy," 227.

[262] Bruce Hoffman, "The Myth of Grass-Roots Terrorism: Why Osama bin Laden Still Matters," *Foreign Affairs* May/June (2008), accessed March 3, 2016, www.foreign affairs.com/reviews/review-essay/2008–05-03/myth-grass-roots-terrorism.

[263] Hoffman, "The Myth." [264] Hoffman, "The Myth."

movement." The second type is "[s]econd-generation failed assimilations" who can become politically radicalized before claiming any religious affinity. The final type is "first-generation migrants who cannot fit into their new society and live life on the margins."[265] These types "share a growing sense of aggrievement and frustration with a perceived war against the Muslim world by the west. This feeling is fueled by events in Iraq, Palestine, and the Balkans."[266] To this Hoffman adds, "it is almost impossible to profile this adversary."[267] This raises the question of whether Hoffman's classification is not undermined by his own arguments. Notwithstanding, Sageman and Hoffman are frequently cited in the literature and a mixture of their two perspectives creates much of the basis for later writings. Nesser summarizes this well: "Leaderless jihad may go too far in interpreting the involvement of young criminals as a sign that ideology does not play an important role. The leader-led model, conversely, may go too far in interpreting al-Qaida's involvement as a sign of strategic sophistication."[268]

Another influential perspective in the literature on radicalization is the rebellion theory. One of the most prominent scholars here is Olivier Roy. To recap, Roy had already proposed in the 1990s that a political radicalization of popular Islam had been taking place within the Muslim world since the 1960s. This is the baseline for his argument about contemporary radicalization in Europe. The Muslim youths drawn to violence have less to do with religious

---

[265] Hoffman, "Radicalisation, Terrorism, and Diasporas," in "The Radicalization of Diasporas and Terrorism: A Joint Conference by the RAND Corporation and the Center for Security Studies," Bruce Hoffman, William Rosenau, Andrew J. Curiel, Doron Zimmermann, RAND National Security Research Division (2007), 3 [1–3].

[266] Hoffman, "Radicalisation," 3. [267] Hoffman, "Radicalisation," 3.

[268] Nesser, *Islamist*, 5. See also Hafez and Mullins, "The Radicalization," 961.

radicalization than a rebellious attitude toward their parents and society.[269] Their motivations "have more to do with rebels searching for meaning than religious radicalization."[270] The key to this revolt, he says, is first of all that these youth have not been taught a culturally rooted religion, which they would have in their country of origin. This is not the case for first-generation immigrants, who supposedly bring with them their culturally rooted religion, nor is it for third-generation immigrants who are "familiar with Islamic modes of expression" in their new society (French society in the quoted text). According to Roy, this explains why there are more Maghrebins than Turks in the radical milieu. In other words, it is the second-generation Maghrebins who are prone to radicalization and terrorism. But if it is not a matter of religious radicalization, why do they choose Islam as an outlet for their rebellion? "Evidently," Roy states, "they pick an identity that, in their eyes, their parents have spoiled"; it is a "nihilist and generational response." Thanks to the exclusive backdrop of Salafist exclusivity, they portray themselves as "more Muslim than Muslims," especially their parents. As for non-Muslim converts, he adds, "[t]hey choose Islam because it is on the market of radical revolt. To join ISIS is a certain path to be able to terrorise."[271] Exactly why Islam is picked on the market of rebellion and not, say, Punk or Goth, and why it would lead to violence and death are not explained. It is as if these young Muslims are somehow predisposed to jihadism.

---

[269] See Olivier Roy, *Globalized Islam: The search for a new ummah* (New York: Columbia University Press, 2004); Olivier Roy, *Enquête de l'Orient perdu : Entretiens avec Jean-Louis Schlegel* (Paris: Seuil, 2014).

[270] Oliveir Roy, "Le djihadisme est une révolte génerationelle et nihilist," *Le Monde* November 24, 2015, accessed February 15, 2016, http://abonnes.lemonde.fr/idees/article/2015/11/24/le-djihadisme-une-revolte-generationnelle-et-nihiliste_4815992_3232.html.

[271] Roy, "Le djihadisme."

Angel Rabas and Cheryl Benard's analysis of what they call "Eurojihad"
is an example of an approach that seeks to converge rebellion theory, psychological perspectives, and a mixed top-down–bottom-up perspective. Drawing
on "most dictionaries," the authors broadly define radicalization "as the process
through which individuals or groups adopt extreme ideas."[272] However, since,
as they argue, radicalization is context dependent, the radicalization in a
European context means "the rejection of the key dimensions of modern
democratic culture that are at the center of the European value system."[273]
These values are "support for democracy and internationally recognized
human rights, gender equality and freedom of worship, respect for diversity,
acceptance of nonsectarian sources of law and opposition to violence as a means
to attain political ends."[274] While they draw on Roy's work, which is interpreted as meaning that "some second-generation Muslims find it difficult to live
within either the traditional culture of their parents or the modern Western
culture of the countries they reside,"[275] the authors state that "structural
variables rarely bear out as proximate causes of terrorism."[276] As with both
Sageman and Hoffman, social alienation is perceived as a matter of perception
among these Muslims and not a social fact. They conclude, moreover, that "the
European Muslim community is divided into two." The first group is made up
of moderates who seek "to integrate into Europe and its values," and the other
group is made up of Salafists who reject both "Western values and the
traditional, culturally bound beliefs of the majority of Europe's Muslims."[277]
However, on one issue these groups seem to converge, at least partly, since
most "Salafis, and even other Muslims, are equivocal on the issue of

[272] Rafas and Benard, *Eurojihad*, 3. [273] Rafas and Benard, *Eurojihad*, 3.
[274] Rafas and Benard, *Eurojihad*, 3. [275] Rafas and Benard, *Eurojihad*, 4.
[276] Rafas and Benard, *Eurojihad*, 2. [277] Rafas and Benard, *Eurojihad*, 4.

terrorism."[278] To the authors, the problem of radicalization thus seems to be rooted in integration, but since these structural explanations are not applicable, the problem of integration appears to reside in the refusal of certain Muslim groups to integrate into European societies. The situation, however, is not hopeless, they say. In Germany, signs of willing integration have been echoed through music: "a surprising number of young rappers and hip-hop artists have merged with an unabashedly pro-integration message."[279] They talk about expressions of "promising, culturally organic developments that bear watching and encouragement."[280] As an example, they take the German rapper Harris, who sings about how he would gladly show the nearest way to the airport for the ones complaining about racism and discrimination in Germany.[281] This rapper made headlines for what critics consider to be far-right and ultranationalist texts.[282] Whether or not shipping immigrants who use the right to free speech to denounce racism and discrimination in their new country of residence is compatible with "European values" is not discussed by the authors, nor is to what degree integration is a suitable conceptual frame for understanding second- or third-generation German citizens.

As becomes clear from these different takes on radicalization, nowhere is the link made explaining why certain young Muslims take up arms. Rather, a group of suspected individuals is created through the intersections of three themes or contexts. These themes are, as Sedgwick notes, security, integration,

---

[278] Rafas and Benard, *Eurojihad*, 30. [279] Rafas and Benard, *Eurojihad*, 176.

[280] Rafas and Benard, *Eurojihad*, 176. [281] CD-reference …

[282] See Stefan Strauss, "Der Rapper Harris von Migrante hierzulande Benehmen – und löst damit eine Debatte aus," *Berliner Zeitung*, October 28 (2010), accessed February 3, 2016, www.berliner-zeitung.de/der-rapper-harris-fordert-von-migranten-hierzulande-benehmen–und-loest-damit-eine-debatte-aus-ein-lied-fuer-deutschland-15035842.

and foreign policy.[283] One problem that emerges is that any definition of radicalization will be dependent on the context given precedence. For example, the sloppy usage of the terms "Salafism" and "jihadism" leads, from a security perspective, to a belief that any sign of a Salafist identity becomes a potential threat. Such a conclusion overlooks distinctions between holding and practicing what might be considered radical views and equating them with violence *to come*.[284] Some scholars, such as Farhad Khosrokhavar who has conducted field-work in French prisons, even argue that Salafism "is the most potent obstacle towards radicalization in the sense that it absorbs many young people's need for a new identity in rupture with society and transforms it into a non-violent sectarian attitude."[285] This is not to say that Khosrokhavar is right and the others are wrong; it is, however, to suggest that when empirical research exists in a field that is painfully lacking thereof, this research should at least be taken into consideration.

Moreover, when radicalization is viewed through the lens of integration, it seems as if blunt generalizations and stereotyping of Muslims are the result.[286] Consider this statement by Rafas and Benard: "Most Salafis, and even other Muslims, are equivocal on the issue of terrorism."[287] To this statement, they add that there is a "pool of radical sympathizers in European Muslim communities."[288] What the basis of these statements is and how the conclusion is drawn are not accounted for. Similarly, Egerton suggests that among "members [sic] of Muslim communities in the West, there is much sympathy, not generally for the militants' methods, but for many of the religio-political claims they make" and that "Muslims in the West broadly share with the militants a

---

[283] Sedgwick, "The Concept," 479. [284] Kundnani, *The Muslims*, 229.
[285] Khosrokhavar, "Radicalization," 304. [286] See further, Hellmich, "Creating."
[287] Rafas and Benard, *Eurojihad*, 30. [288] Rafas and Benard, *Eurojihad*, 54.

belief that the West is at best unfair in its dealings with Islam and Muslims."[289] No polls, interviews, or other observations are accounted for. Islam here appears as a self-explicatory category.

A similar problem is found in Roy's theory of rebellion and dual identity. As Orla Lynch notes, Roy's argument that intergenerational conflicts appear within immigrant families is well supported in academic research.[290] The causal relation between radicalization and rebellion "remains untested" even as it "exists unquestioned as evidence of the potential for radicalisation inherent in all Muslim youth."[291] Regarding the theory of dual identity, second and to some degree third generations of Muslim immigrants

> are unable to reconcile their new Western identity with their national heritage or ethnic identity, and are thus constantly and problematically managing two sets of norms. Using such a claim, there is then a crude relationship suggested between identity confusion and vulnerability to radicalisation given the supposed need for Muslim youth from immigrant families to seek out an identity based on radical interpretations of Islam. The complexity of identity theory from sociology and psychology is not reflected in any meaningful way in this discussion and evidence from the individuals at the centre of this debate is absent.[292]

Now, even if Roy were to be correct in his theories, why they lead to violence is not explained. Kundnani sees a similar problem in Sageman's writings. Kundnani argues that even if Sageman's model offers "a plausible explanation

---

[289] Egerton, *Jihad*, 135.

[290] Orla Lynch, "British Muslim Youth: Radicalisation, terrorism and the construction of the 'other,'" *Critical Studies on Terrorism* 6(2) (2013), 244 [241–261].

[291] Lynch, "British," 244. [292] Lynch, "British," 244.

of how radical ideas circulate, it has nothing to say on what causes supporters of such ideas to favor violence over other means of advancing their cause."[293] This leads the reader to draw the conclusion that "the question of violence can only be answered by assuming certain ideologies are inherently violent. The picture is one in which the Salafi script is already a predisposition to violence that only needs a friendship dynamic to activate it."[294] In the case of Sageman and Roy, it appears as if the will to extract "religion" from the path to terrorism actually brings in a culturalized explicatory model of Islam through the backdoor.

A final remark about radicalization is how it not only ascribes an explicatory factor to Islam, but it also produces notions of the normal and the abnormal. As Sedgwick notes, a dictionary definition of "radical" is a category that can be equated with "extremist," which is the opposite of "moderate," meaning that a continuum between the two categories can be sketched.[295] Viewed from this perspective, two important questions need to be posed: "Where does the moderate section of the continuum lie?" and "What continuum should be considered in the first place?"[296] Khosrokhavar suggests that "radicalization does not only apply to Islamic extremism"; it is a more general process "by which an individual or a group adopts a violent form of action as a consequence of extreme political, social or religious ideologies questioning the prevailing social, cultural and political order."[297] As such, it "encompasses other phenomena: the neo-Nazi movement, radical anti-abortion activism or so-called 'eco-terrorism.'"[298] Not only could the list be extended to incorporate all kinds of antiestablishment movements and activists, by taking Sedgwick's notion of continuum into consideration, we see that radicalization becomes dependent on the prevailing social, cultural, and political hegemony that depicts

[293] Kundnani, *The Muslims*, 229. [294] Kundnani, *The Muslims*, 229.
[295] Sedgwick, "The Concept," 482. [296] Sedgwick, "The Concept," 482.
[297] Khosrokhavar, "Radicalization," 286. [298] Khosrokhavar, "Radicalization," 286.

itself as the norm. As an analytical category, it thus becomes, as Sedgewick notes, "a source of confusion."[299]

Fighting Tomorrow's Terrorists Today

To what degree 9/11 was the epitome of a new arena dominated by religious terrorism is debated in the field of terrorism studies. However, few scholars disagree that 9/11 was the beginning of a new era for counterterrorism. One of the lessons learned from previous counterterrorism measures is that the proportionality of the risk ascribed to terrorism vis-à-vis the probability of an actual attack tends to be widely exaggerated, leading to a mismatched risk assessment with severe backfire effects.[300] The post-9/11 United States provides some examples. Arjun Chowdhury and Scott Fitzsimmons point to how the Bush administration appeared to ignore al-Qaida's "stated political objectives," such as withdrawal of US troops from Saudi Arabia, and argued that al-Qaida's "violent attacks against American targets proved that it sought the destruction of the American political system and way of life."[301] The symbolic threat of terrorism appeared to be given precedence over al-Qaida's material

---

[299] Sedgewick, "The Concept," title.

[300] See Konstantinos Drakos and Catherine Mueller, "On the Determinants of Terrorism Risk Concern in Europe," *Defence and Peace Economics* 25(3) (2014), 291 [291–310]; Lars Lindekilde, "A Typology of Backfire Mechanisms: How soft and hard forms of state repression can have perverse effects in the field of counterterrorism," in *Dynamics of Political Violence: A process-oriented perspective on radicalisation and the escalation of political conflict*, eds. Lorenzo Bosi, Chares Demetriou, and Stefan Malthaner (Surrey: Ashgate, 2012), 51–70.

[301] Arjun Chowdhury and Scott Fitzsimmons, "Effective but Inefficient: Understanding the costs of counterterrorism," *Critical Studies on Terrorism* 6(3) (2013), 450–451 [447–456].

capabilities: "Despite the comparatively limited material capabilities of the terrorist groups involved, leaders represented them as vital symbolic contests – wars of national survival – that warranted concerted military effort."[302] The new theory of terrorism held sway and made an ontological and epistemological backbone for the portrayal of a civilizational clash between the Free World and the Axis of Evil. Fighting evil with diplomacy was useless, the argument went.[303] Arbitrary detentions without trials, the drone program killing fifty civilians for every "strategic target," extrajudicial killings, torture, mass surveillance, and the whole bundle of repressive and securitizing measures installed post-9/11 have had devastating effects in terms of human rights, civil liberties, and peace.[304] Meanwhile, Richard Jackson points out, it is "known" that "the violent suppression of terrorism is less effective than conciliation-oriented approaches such as direct dialogue."[305] Dialogue and understanding have not been the *modus operandi* post-9/11. In 2006, for example, out of 12,000 agents, the FBI had just 33 special agents with a proficiency in Arabic. The Department of Homeland Security and the CIA

---

[302] Chowdhury and Fitzsimmons, "Effective," 452.

[303] For a critical introduction, see Carl Miller, "Is It Possible and Preferable to Negotiate with Terrorists?" *Defence Studies* 11(1) (2011), 145–185. For an example of the argument, see Jan Kallberg andBhavani Thuraisingham, "After the 'War on Terror'—how to maintain long-range terrorist deterrence," *Journal of Policing, Intelligence and Counter Terrorism* 9(1) (2014), 19–31.

[304] Keith Patrick Dear, "Beheading the Hydra? Does killing terrorist or insurgent leaders work?" *Defence Studies* 13(3) (2013), 293–337; Liz Fekete, "All in the Name of Security," in *Beyond September 11: An anthology of dissent*, ed. Phil Scraton (London and Sterling: Pluto Press, 2002), 102–107; Joseba Zulaika, "Drones, Witches and Other Flying Objects: The force of fantasy in US counterterrorism," *Critical Studies on Terrorism* 5(1) (2012), 51–68.

[305] Richard Jackson, "The Epistemological Crisis of Counterterrorism," *Critical Studies on Terrorism* 8(1) (2015), 45 [33–54].

even appear to have ruled out employing native Arabic speakers since they were seen as security risks. This is not only discriminatory; it also hampers the efficacy of counterintelligence work. As Jarret Brachman points out, "Western, school-trained Arabic speakers" are "significantly less able to handle multiple dialects and idioms."[306] One of the main problems with counterterrorism measures is that they are not only undermining the values and rights that the Free World supposedly fights for "over there," they also run the risk of undermining these values "here" as well. Portraying the near political and social future in absolutist terms fueled by a climate of fear seems to serve strong leaders and hard-line policies and brings about a willingness to give up civil liberties to combat terrorism.[307]

To what degree the EU and its member states have learned from the accumulated knowledge of the harmful effects of certain US counterterrorism measures post-9/11 is up for debate.[308] The last major attacks on European soil

[306] Jarret M. Brachman, *Global Jihadism: Theory and practice* (London and New York: Routledge, 2009), 185.

[307] See Bleich, Erik, "State Responses to 'Muslim' Violence: A comparison of six West European countries," *Journal of Ethnic and Migration Studies* 35(3) (2009), 361–379; Henar Criado, "What Makes Terrorism Salient? Terrorist Strategies, Political Competition, and Public Opinion," *Terrorism and Political Violence*, 20(3) (2015) [online first].

[308] See Jackson, "The Epistemological." For literature on radicalization and deradi-calization, see Rober J. Arts and Louise Richardson, eds., *Democracy and Counterterrorism: Lessons from the past* (Washington, DC: United States Institute of Peace, 2007); Omar Ashour, *The De-Radicalization of Jihadists: Transforming armed Islamist movements* (London and New York: Routledge, 2009); Tore Bjorgo and John Horgan, *Leaving Terrorism Behind: Individual and collective disengage-ment* (London and New York: Routledge, 2009); Frank Foley, *Countering Terrorism in Britain and France: Institutions, norms and the shadow of the past* (Cambridge: Cambridge University Press, 2013).

suggests otherwise. For example, responding to the two attacks in Paris in 2015, French state leaders echoed the war cries of the Bush administration, installed a state of emergency, and pushed for more intrusive and securitizing measures, resulting in thousands of arbitrary detentions, interrogation of citizens as young as eight years old, flash trials, and incarcerations based on ethnic and religious profiling.[309] In a situation where terrorism is construed as an omnipresent and perpetual threat or where the "homegrown" radicalized jihadi might be your own neighbor, children's friend, or student, countermeasures are also forged in a similar matter. Politics and law are merging in a "fuzzy middle zone," to quote Mathew Stone et al., where the "real 'field of pain and death,' upon which legality is predicated, is no longer merely the courtroom, but also the planning office, the social security department, the job centre."[310] Academia can be added to this but with one distinction between mainstream and critical scholars. Claire Lyness shows that Robert Pape's definition of terrorism is taken from the US State Department document "Patterns of Global Terrorism 2003."[311] According to Pape, there is no reason to broaden such a definition to include state terrorism since "such a definition would distract attention from what policy makers would most like to know: how to combat the threat posed by non-state actors to the national security of the United States and our allies."[312] In this vein, David Miller and Tom Mills suggest: "The ideas prominent in orthodox terrorism studies, and often the theorists themselves, have strong

---

[309] See Didier Fassin, "Short Cuts," *London Review of Books* 38(5) (2016), 23; Nilsson, "Where's."

[310] Matthew Stone, Illan rua Wall, and Costas Douzinas, "Introduction: Law, politics and the political," in *New Critical Legal Thinking*, eds. Matthew Stone, Illan rua Wall, and Costas Douzinas (New York: Routledge, 2012), 1–2 [1–8].

[311] Claire Lyness, "Governing the Suicide Bomber: Reading terrorism studies as governmentality," *Critical Studies on Terrorism* 7(1) (2014), 84 [79–96].

[312] Pape in Lyness, "Governing," 84.

roots in counterinsurgency doctrine and practice. Orthodox terrorism experts are, in other words, ideologically committed and practically engaged in supporting Western state power."[313] If *mainstream* scholars work in tandem with policy makers to develop more effective countermeasures, *critical* scholars set out to understand "the extent to which counterterrorism contributes to the promotion and perpetuation of terrorism."[314] At least that is the expressed ambition.

This section serves as an introduction to issues concerning the intersection of academia, law, and politics. Focus is placed on the EU's counterterrorism measures. In the first part of the section, I discuss the overarching legal and institutional counterterrorism framework. The section gives a brief background of the development of these measures, an insight into the definition of terrorism as a threat, and finally an overview of some of the most important institutions working with counterterrorism. In the second part, I turn to discuss counter-radicalization as a specific measure in the EU counterterrorism apparatus. Counter-radicalization is often described as a softer countermeasurement within the broader counterterrorism apparatus and focuses explicitly on preventing EU citizens from turning into full-blown "terrorists."

A Paper Tiger?

Terrorism has been part of EU lingua for decades. Separatist movements such as the Corsican *Fronte di Liberazione Naziunale Corsu* (FLNC)[315] has, since its

---

[313] David Miller and Tom Mills, "The Terror Experts and the Mainstream Media: The expert nexus and its dominance in the news media," *Critical Studies on Terrorism* 2(3) (2009), 414–415 [414–437].

[314] Zulaika, "Drones," 51.

[315] See Javier Argomaniz, Oldrich Bures, and Christian Kaunert, "A Decade of EU Counter-Terrorism and Intelligence: A critical assessment," *Intelligence and National Security* (2015) 30(2–3), 191–206.

formation in 1975, carried out more than 10,000 attacks, killed more than 220 state officials, mainly security personnel, and injured thousands.[316] However, in stark contrast to Islamic terrorism, violence by the FLNC does not attract media attention.[317] In line with the theory of new terrorism, 9/11 was the birth of a different kind of threat, and the attributed importance to the threat posed by terrorism changed with 9/11.[318] As Tony Bunyan puts it, 9/11 came "to hasten and exacerbate a process that was already under way – to hothouse it, as it were."[319]

The current EU counterterrorism's strategic objectives were laid down in the European Union Counter-Terrorism Strategy in 2005 as a response to Madrid and London.[320] It is divided into four subject areas. The first is "prevent," with the aim to "prevent people turning to terrorism by tackling root causes which can lead to radicalization and recruitment." The second is "protect," which aims at protecting "citizens and infrastructure" by improving "security of borders, transport and critical infrastructure." The third subject

---

[316] Shaun Gregory, "France and the War on Terrorism," *Terrorism and Political Violence* 15(1) (2003), 126 [124–147].

[317] Andreas Michael Hoffbauer, "Competing Claims: When Do Corsican Nationalists Gain Foreign News Coverage?" *Terrorism and Political Violence* 23(4) (2011), 623 [623–641].

[318] Monica Den Boer and Irina Wiegand, "From Convergence to Deep Integration: Evaluating the Impact of EU Counter-Terrorism Strategies on Domestic Arenas," *Intelligence and National Security*, 30(2–3) (2015), 380 [377–401].

[319] Tony Bunyan, "Just Over the Horizon – the Surveillance Society and the State in the EU," *Race & Class* 51(3) (2010), 11 [1–12]. Also see Rygiel, Kim, "Citizenship as Government: Disciplining populations post-9/11," in *Illusions of Control: Discipline and punishment in global politics*, ed. Janie Leatherman (New York: Palgrave Macmillan, 2008), 85 [85–110].

[320] Argomaniz et al., "A Decade," 196.

area, "pursue," targets "terrorists across borders and globally" with the aim of impeding, disrupting, and "bring[ing] terrorists to justice." Finally, "respond" aims at managing and minimizing "in the spirit of solidarity," to improve capabilities to deal with the aftermath, the coordination, and the needs of victims after an attack.[321]

Cooperation and Convergence

The 2005 EU Counter-Terrorism Strategy is not the first attempt to put in writing a counterterrorist strategy. In 1975, EC member states created the intergovernmental cooperation framework *Terrorisme, radicalisme et violence international* (TREVI).[322] The impact of TREVI was, however, minimal; it was after 9/11 that the EU first came to develop a more coherent counterterrorism program. Bakker points out that in the wake of the attacks, the European Commission published a "Proposal for a Council Framework Decision on Combating Terrorism" (September 19, 2001) and organized an extraordinary European Council meeting that lead to "a plan of action that included, amongst others, strengthening air security and enhancing police and judicial cooperation."[323] In October, a second meeting was held and led to a program proposing nearly eighty counterterrorism measures. "These two gatherings in the immediate aftermath of 9/11 were the beginning of a long list of meetings, and an 'Anti-terrorism Roadmap' – a plan of concrete counter-terrorism actions

---

[321] Council of the European Union, "European Union Counter-Terrorism Strategy," November 30, 2005, 3, accessed March 3, 2016, http://register.consilium.europa .eu/doc/srv?l=EN&f=ST%2014469%202005%20REV%204.

[322] Jörg Monar, "Common Threat and Common Response? The European Union's counter-terrorism strategy and its problems," *Government and Opposition* 42(3) (2007), 292 [292–313].

[323] Bakker, "EU," 289–290.

for the EU," to quote Bakker. The attacks, moreover, led to an acceleration "of the ratification of existing legislation by member states."[324]

In 2002, the Council Framework Decision on Combating Terrorism was put in place.[325] When Gijs de Vries was appointed as the first EU counter-terrorism coordinator (CTC) in 2004, an important step was taken.[326] By then, Jörg Monar points out, the degree of integration by the EU members laid out the framework for more far-reaching counterterrorism measures.[327] According to Mackenzie et al., the EU CTC's main occupations are (a) "coordinating the counter-terrorism work of the Justice and Home Affairs Council"; (b) "maintaining an overview of the relevant EU instruments in this area; (c) "ensuring effective follow-up of Council decisions; (d) "monitoring the implementation of the EU Counter-terrorism Strategy, including making reports to the Council"; (e) fostering better communication between the EU and third countries; and (f) ensuring that the EU plays an active role in the fight against terrorism as a whole."[328] The impact of the coordinator is contested, to say the least. As Mackenzie et al. point out, leading scholars have criticized the EU CTC for lacking "any real power to force member states to cooperate," that it depends on "goodwill," that it "has virtually no power, apart from that of persuasion," and that it is "a political half-way house … lambasted as a lame duck."[329] Mackenzie et al. however state that this critique "tend[s] to neglect to a significant extent the external dimension of his activities (the EU CTC), that is, the tasks that concern third countries and bodies, beyond the EU."[330]

---

[324] Bakker, "EU," 290.
[325] http://eur-lex.europa.eu/legal-content/EN/TXT/PDF/?uri=CELEX:32002F04 75&from=EN.
[326] See Argomaniz et al., "A Decade," 197. [327] Monar, "Common," 292.
[328] Mackenzie et al., "The European," 328–329.
[329] Mackenzie et al., The European," 326.
[330] Mackenzie et al., "The European," 326.

Moreover The Hague Program of 2005, with the goal of setting out the 10 most central priorities regarding the area of freedom, security, and justice within the EU for the five coming years, listed anti-terrorist measures as number two.[331] The program states the following:

> A comprehensive response to terrorism is the only way to combat it effectively. The approach must be integrated and coherent. The Commission emphasises the need for terrorism prevention and exchanging information. Its intention is to support Member States in their fight against terrorism by focusing on terrorism recruitment and financing, prevention, risk analysis, protection of vulnerable infrastructure and consequence management.[332]

The Stockholm Program of 2010 has further developed guidelines that have since been referred to as the European Area of Freedom Security and Justice (AFSJ).[333] At this more general level, Monica den Boer and Irina Wiegand conclude that the EU "has unfolded a roadmap for counterterrorism measures and an itinerary of actions to be undertaken by the Member States" where "EU

---

[331] Edwin Bakker, "EU Counter-radicalization Policies: A comprehensive and consistent approach?," *Intelligence and National Security* 30(2–3) (2015), 281–305 [online].

[332] Communication from the Commission to the Council and the European Parliament, "The Hague Programme: Ten priorities for the next five years. The Partnership for European renewal in the field of Freedom, Security and Justice," May 10, 2005, accessed March 10, 2016, http://eur-lex.europa.eu/legal-content/PL/TXT/?uri=URISERV:l16002.

[333] Raphael Bossong, "EU Cooperation on Terrorism Prevention and Violent Radicalization: Frustrated ambitions or new forms of EU security governance?" *Cambridge Review of International Affairs* 27(1) (2014), 66 [66–82].

counter-terrorism can be perceived as a form of multi-level governance in which the EU is one player amidst several others."[334] However, the efficiency and efficacy of these EU counterterrorism measures have been criticized, not least for being ambiguous and unsuccessful in their implementation.[335] Monar, for example, argues that the EU in this regard is based more "on cooperation and coordination than on any form of integration."[336] "The member states are in fact much better at agreeing on comprehensive packages of measures," Monar says, "than at effectively implementing them afterwards."[337] Another issue concerns the EU's chances to impact national anti-terrorism measures. Den Boer and Wiegard state: "In terms of governance, the EU can only take recourse to coordination powers, principally through the EU Counter-Terrorism Coordinator. Hence, potential convergence between national counter-terrorism systems may result from intergovernmental initiatives rather than from top-down steering through supranational governance."[338] However, this situation is, according to den Boer and Wiegand, slowly changing. The Treaty of Lisbon has given the Commission, the Parliament, and the Court of Justice more powers "in the area of criminal justice cooperation and counter-terrorism than ever before."[339] Anti-terrorism measures and institutions such as Europol, Eurojust, CTC, the European Arrest Warrant, the EU Data Retention Directive, the Schengen Information System, have brought about advances in integration in this regard.[340] Notwithstanding, the authors conclude that the EU has clearly "not replaced Member States in this domain, and limitations of its legal competences,

[334] Den Boer and Wiegand, "From," 377. [335] Bossong, "EU," 66.
[336] Monar, "Common," 310. [337] Monar, "Common," 310.
[338] Den Boer and Wiegard, "From," 378. [339] Den Boer and Wiegard, "From," 378.
[340] Den Boer and Wiegard, "From," 383.

institutional framework and internal counterterrorism measures" have given rise to the equation of the EU anti-terrorism measures with a "paper tiger."[341]

Defining the Threat

Monar states that the EU's counterterrorism measures "constitute an interesting attempt at Europeanizing and responding to a threat that is usually presented only either as a national or global one."[342] This raises one central aspect of any counterterrorism apparatus: defining what it is supposed to counter. Monar points out how the development of Framework Decision of 2002 called for "a need to agree on the perception of a more specific threat as regards the Union in order to justify this piece of legislation, which was seen by some as a potential threat to civil liberties."[343] The Framework states that terrorism "constitutes one of the most serious violations" against the EU principles of "the universal values of human dignity, liberty, equality and solidarity, respect for human rights and fundamental freedoms" and, moreover, "the principle of democracy and the principle of the rule of law."[344] These declarations refer back to the La Gomera Declaration of 1995, which states, among other things, that terrorism "constitutes a threat to democracy, to the free exercise of human rights and to economic and social development, from which no Member State of the European Union can be regarded as

---

[341] Jörg Monar, "The EU as an International Counter-terrorism Actor: Progress and constraints," *Intelligence and National Security* 30(2–3) (2015), 335 [333–356].

[342] Monar, "Common," 293. [343] Monar, "Common," 294.

[344] The Council of the European Union, "Council Framework Decision on Combating Terrorism," June 13, 2002, accessed March 10, 2016, http://eur-lex.europa.eu/legal-content/EN/TXT/PDF/?uri=CELEX:32002F0475&from=EN.

exempt."[345] The most extensive definition was laid down in the European Union's Framework Decision on Combating Terrorism of 2002:

> [A]s offences under national law, which, given their nature or context, may seriously damage a country or an international organisation where committed with the aim of: [a] seriously intimidating a population, or [b] unduly compelling a Government or international organisation to perform or abstain from performing any act, or [c] seriously destabilising or destroying the fundamental political, constitutional, economic or social structures of a country or an international organisation.

The document specifies a number of "terrorist offences":

> (a) attacks upon a person's life which may cause death; (b) attacks upon the physical integrity of a person; (c) kidnapping or hostage taking; (d) causing extensive destruction to a Government or public facility, a transport system, an infrastructure facility, including an information system, a fixed platform located on the continental shelf, a public place or private property likely to endanger human life or result in major economic loss; (e) seizure of aircraft, ships or other means of public or goods transport; (f) manufacture, possession, acquisition, transport, supply or use of weapons, explosives or of

---

[345] European Parliament, "Madrid European Council Presidency Conclusions: Annexes 1–5," December 15–16, 1995, accessed March 10, 2016, www.europarl .europa.eu/summits/mad2_en.htm#annex3.

nuclear, biological or chemical weapons, as well as research into, and development of, biological and chemical weapons; (g) release of dangerous substances, or causing fires, floods or explosions the effect of which is to endanger human life; (h) interfering with or disrupting the supply of water, power or any other fundamental natural resource the effect of which is to endanger human life; (i) threatening to commit any of the acts listed in (a) to (h).

Moreover, the European Union Strategy for Combating Radicalization and Recruitment to Terrorism of 2005 declares that "the terrorism perpetrated by Al-Qa'ida and extremists inspired by Al-Qa'ida has become the main terrorist threat to the Union." It recognized that while "other types of terrorism ... pose a serious threat to EU citizens, the Union's response to radicalization and recruitment focuses on this type of terrorism."[346]

Summarizing the threat assessment, Monar argues that the EU has arrived at a definition that consists "of seven principle elements": (a) terrorism post-9/11 poses a threat against citizens as well as the foundations of the EU and its member states; (b) the threat is "marked by the enhanced resources of terrorists and their increasing willingness to use massive violence to induce mass casualties; (c) the threat is not only posed by al-Qaida "but also by those inspired by it, who operate from within the EU"; (d) the threat is not isolated from other "international threats" such as "the proliferation of weapons of mass destruction, state failure and organized crime"; (e) the threat "is rooted in a

---

[346] Council of the European Union, "The European Union Strategy for Combating Radicalisation and Recruitement to Terrorism," November 24, 2005, accessed March 10, 2016, http://register.consilium.europa.eu/doc/srv?l=EN&f=ST% 2014781%202005%20REV%201.

complex set of causes," including "political, religious, cultural, social"; (f) a sensitivity not to portray the threat as an "Islamic" one, and that "any idea of terrorism as a clash with Islam and the Muslim world must be rejected"; and (g) that the "EU is particularly vulnerable to this threat because of its 'openness' as an area without internal borders."[347]

Combating the Threat

Today the EU fights terrorism through a broad range of institutions. In this section, I present some of the most significant areas: surveillance, policing, finance, boarder control, and propaganda. The majority of these measures are, as noted earlier, based on convergence that is harmonization and cooperation by the member states rather than marking out a proper EU antiterrorist brigade.

The EU Intelligence Analysis Center (INTCEN) is the most secretive of these institutions.[348] It is part of the EU External Action Service (EEAS). INTCEN is the EU civilian intelligence function, and it provides security and threat analysis and assessments for EU decision makers.[349] INTCEN does not collect its own source material but collates intelligence gathered by other member states and EU allies. As such, INTCEN functions as an analytical meta-forum for the member states' security services. According to den Boer, this aspect of INTCEN is "revolutionary," since it has opened the road for multidisciplinary intelligence exchange, in particular between military and civil security authorities.[350]

---

[347] Monar, "Common," 298.

[348] Until 2012, it was called the EU Situation Centre (SITCEN).

[349] Intelligence Analysis Centre, "EU INTCEN Fact-Sheet, February 5, 2015, accessed March 10, 2016, http://eeas.europa.eu/factsheets/docs/20150206_factshee t_eu_intcen_en.pdf.

[350] Den Boer, "Counter-Terrorism," 410.

The European Police Office (Europol) is the policing branch of the EU. It was created in 1992 but had no explicitly stated objective to combat terrorism until the Council Decision of April 6, 2009. Today its operational activities are listed in the areas of illicit drugs, human trafficking, cyber crime, intellectual property rights violation, cigarette smuggling, counterfeit, VAT fraud, money laundering and asset tracing, mobile organized crime groups, outlaw motor-cycle gangs, and finally terrorism. The stated objective of Europol is "to support and strengthen action by the competent authorities of the Member States and their mutual cooperation in preventing and combating organised crime, terrorism and other forms of serious crime affecting two or more Member States."[351] According to den Boer, Europol "has played a leading role in the development of methods and instruments for reliable intelligence-exchange" through, among other means, the European Crime Intelligence Model (ECIM); the Organized Crime Threat Assessment (OCTA); the Annual Situation and Trends Report (TE-SAT); and, since 2016, the European Counter Terrorism Center (ECTC).[352] The ECTC has four over-arching functions: to be an information hub for counterterrorism; to provide operational support, coordination, and expertise; to fight terrorist and violent online content; and to give strategic support capability to the member states.[353]

Europol has also been given a significant role in the EU and US Terrorist Finance Tracking agreement (TFTP). Oldrich Bures explains that the logic of combating terrorist financing is straightforward: "[I]f the money

---

[351] The Council of the Euroepan Union, "Council Decision Establishing the European Police Office (Europol)," *Official Journal of the European Union*, 371/JHA (April 6, 2009), L 121/39.

[352] Den Boer, "Counter-Terrorism," 406.

[353] Europol, "ECTC Infograph," accessed March 10, 2016, www.europol.europa.eu/content/ectc.

can be shut down, so can the terrorist activities that it was meant to finance."[354] This is why, Bures states, "efforts to disrupt, deter and dismantle terrorist financing networks have become the key elements of the EU's post-9/11 counterterrorism policy."[355]

The Council of Europe Convention on the Prevention of Terrorism of 2005 sets out the guidelines on propaganda or the incitement to terrorism. The Convention urges member states to "take effective measures to prevent terrorism and to counter, in particular, public provocation to commit terrorist offences and recruitment and training for terrorism."[356] It specifies that "public provocation to commit a terrorist offence" refers to "the distribution, or otherwise making available, of a message to the public, with the intent to incite the commission of a terrorist offence" that "causes a danger that one or more such offences may be committed."[357] As Ben Saul shows, in the Explanatory Report on Council of Europe Convention on the Prevention of Terrorism, a discussion of how incitement, or the imperfectly commensurate *apologie* in French, was to be understood. Since it sought to cover "the public expression of praise, support, or justification of terrorism," it was "broader than ordinary incitement to commit a crime (including terrorism), which is already an offence

---

[354] Oldrich Bures, "Ten Years of EU's Fight against Terrorist Financing: A critical assessment," *Intelligence and National Security* 30(2–3) (2015), 207 [207–233]. [Council of the European Union, Revised Strategy on Terrorist Financing. 11778/08, 17.7.2008, p. 7, http://register.consilium.europa.eu/pdf/en/08/st11/st11778-re01.en08.pdf].

[355] Bures, "Ten," 207. Also see Stephen Kingah and Marieke Zwartjes, "Regulating Money Laundering for Terrorism Financing: EU–US transnational policy networks and the financial action task force," *Contemporary Politics* 21(3) (2015), 345 [341–353].

[356] The Convention, 1. [357] The Convention, 3.

in many European (and common law) countries."[358] Saul states that although the "drafters were conscious that criminalising incitement or apologie might interfere in freedom of expression," they "argued that it could still constitute a legitimate restriction under human rights law."[359] Examples of indirect incitement or *apologie* were held as "public provocation" and included "presenting a terrorist offence as necessary and justified," and "the dissemination of messages praising the perpetrator of an attack, the denigration of victims, calls for funding of terrorist organisations or other similar behaviour."[360] During the past decade, incitement laws have been implemented to condemn and expel a small number of Islamic clerics and individuals.[361] To strengthen its arm, Europol set up the EU Internet Referral Unit (IRU) to combat terrorist propaganda and related violent extremist activities on the Internet in July 2015.[362]

One of the core principles of the EU is freedom of movement, as specified in the Schengen Agreement, which, through border-control cooperation, has sought to dismantle the internal borders while strengthening the external ones. The Schengen Information System (SIS) is a large-scale system with the purpose of monitoring third-country-nationals' travels into the Schengen Area, to enable law enforcement cooperation, and to facilitate vehicle registration.[363] Another important agency regarding border controls is

---

[358] Ben Saul, "Speaking of Terror: Criminalising incitement to violence," *UNSW Law Journal* 28(3) (2008), 869 [868–886].

[359] Saul, "Speaking," 869. [360] Saul, "Speaking," 869.

[361] See Bleich, "State," 366; Nilsson, "Where's."

[362] See Europol, "News," July 7, 2015, accessed March 31, 2016, http://ec.europa.eu/dgs/home-affairs/what-is-new/news/news/2015/20150701_01_en.htm.

[363] European Parliament and Council, "Regulation (EC) of the European Parliament and of the Council on the Establishment, Operation and Use of the Second-generation Schengen Information System (SIS II)," no. 1987/2006, December 20,

Frontex. In 2004, Frontex was set up to facilitate and converge the member states' work in controlling the external borders. As den Boer states, "the role of Frontex in counter-terrorism is secondary as it is primarily responsible for monitoring migratory movements into the EU."[364] However, regarding border management,

> it has become responsible for the exchange of information and the surveillance of large groups of the European population. This "logic of control" has been unfolded over a range of activities, including the anticipation of emergency situations at borders, the prediction of futures, policing through knowledge and surveillance, and the functioning on the basis of confidentiality.[365]

Even though the EU has developed a whole apparatus of converging and cooperative measures to combat terrorism, Bossong states, "significant evaluations in counterterrorism remain dependent on national policy-making structures."[366]

A Paper Tiger with a Bite?

The timing of these new counterterrorism measures is worth bringing to the fore since published Europol data suggests that "there is a decreasing trend of attacks attributed to ethno-nationalist terrorist groups, a category that accounts for the vast majority of all terrorist incidents in Europe."[367] It appears that

2006, accessed March 10, 2016, http://eur-lex.europa.eu/legal-content/EN/TXT/?uri=URISERV:l14544.

[364] Den Boer, "Counter-Terrorism," 409. [365] Den Boer, "Counter-Terrorism."
[366] Bossong, "EU," 76. [367] Argomaniz et al., "A Decade," 203–204.

although the EU makes ostentatious efforts not to single out Islamic terrorism, it regards it as a more serious threat and responds to it with tougher measures. Specific measures targeting Islamic terrorism and its effect will be discussed in the following section. For now, however, it is important to bring up the recurring question of security and liberty, which has been much discussed by mainstream scholars and by EU institutions themselves. For example, the European Parliament 2011 LIBE Committee Report raised concerns regarding mass surveillance, such as "large-scale collection of personal data, detection and identification technologies, tracking and tracing, data mining and profiling, risk assessment and behavioural analysis," that are measures "used for the purpose of preventing terrorism."[368] In this regard Monar states that while "the absence of any law enforcement powers 'protects' the EU largely against the risk of infringing directly the civil liberties and human rights of individuals," EU anti-terrorism measures "can have a significant negative impact on civil liberties and human rights," since it can, in the long run, "lead to more controversial restrictive measures at the national level."[369] Tony Bunyan even argues that "the EU and its member states are, today, set on a path which will, in just a few years time, turn this into the most surveilled, monitored region in the world."[370]

Winning Hearts and Minds

As stated earlier, the attacks in Madrid and London accelerated and transformed the EU counterterrorism apparatus in many ways, in particular, in regard to how root causes of terrorism were perceived. Bakker argues that "despite the

---

[368] Argomaniz et al., "A Decade," 200.

[369] Cited in Monar, "Common," 309. Also see Tuomas Ojanen, "Terrorist Profiling: Human rights concerns," *Critical Studies on Terrorism* 3(2) (2010), 296 [295–312].

[370] Bunyan, "Just," 1.

fact that violent radicalization is not new to Europe, the EU policies in this field are rather new."[371] From having talked about "Islamic radicalism" and its sibling categories,[372] radicalization quickly became a key to assess "why the bomb went off." Research on radicalization and the EU is rather sparse, both regarding mainstream and critical approaches.[373] However, the picture is different when it comes to regions and specific member states.[374] The category itself starts being used in the EU after Madrid and London. According to Magnus Hörnqvist and Janne Flyghed, it was "authoritatively put into circulation by the EU Commission" in 2005, which turned it into "the starting point for the extensive discussion of the mechanisms behind terrorism that will be analysed in this article."[375] As Lars Lindekilde states, this new policy area essentially identified "radicalisation, particularly among young Muslims, as a growing social and

---

[371] Bakker, "EU," 304. [372] Ragazzi, *Vers*, 4.

[373] Lindekilde, "Introduction," 336. On the effectiveness see ... include Mythen et al. 2009, Schiffauer 2009, Heath- Kelly 2011, Lindekilde 2012b

[374] For regional European analysis, see Stefano Bonino, "Policing Strategies against Islamic Terrorism in the UK after 9/11: The socio-political realities for British Muslims," *Journal of Muslim Minority Affairs* 32:1 (2012), 5–31; Mohammed Elshimi, "De-radicalisation Interventions as Technologies of the Self: A Foucauldian analysis," *Critical Studies on Terrorism* 8:1 (2015), 110–129; Lasse Lindekilde, "Introduction: Assessing the effectiveness of counter-radicalisation policies in northwestern Europe," *Critical Studies on Terrorism* 5(3) (2012), 335–344; Therese O'Toole, Daniel Nilsson DeHanas, and Tariq Modood, "Balancing Tolerance, Security and Muslim Engagement in the United Kingdom: The impact of the 'Prevent' agenda," *Critical Studies on Terrorism* 5:3 (2012), 373–389; Ragazzi, *Vers*.

[375] Magnus Hörnqvist and Janne Flyghed, "Exclusion or Culture? The rise and the ambiguity of the radicalisation debate," *Critical Studies on Terrorism* 5(3) (2012), 319 [319–334].

security problem to which governments must attend in a timely manner in order to prevent radicalisation processes from taking hold."[376]

Framing Radicalization

Bakker identifies the key question of radicalization as it is posed within the EU to be as follows: "When, why and how do certain individuals become radicalized to the point of being willing to commit acts of terrorism, and what can be done about it?"[377] Answers to this question were sought by a number of EU agencies and working groups. As Bossong states, the European Council saw a need for a new type of counterterrorism that was more adapted to fighting radicalization and seen to be trying to stake out a new path for EU counter-terrorism policy. However, as Bossong points out, how to perceive radicalization was not self-evident. Was it a matter of bottom-up processes, as some scholars thought, or top-down recruitment, as others held? The Expert Group on Violent Radicalization launched by the European Commission in 2006 sought to give guidance.[378] The group was made up of leading scholars within the field of terrorism studies, such as Donatella della Porta, Farhad Khosrokhavar, Magnus Ranstorp, Fernando Reinares, Alex O. Schmid, and Gijs de Vries. The Expert Group defined radicalization as a "phased process" or a "process of socialization" leading up to the use of violence, and that, in "the framework of this concise Report, 'violent radicalisation' often refers to radicalisation to jihadist violence or jihadist terrorism."[379]

---

[376] Lindekilde, "Introduction," 335. [377] Bakker, "EU," 283.

[378] The European Commission's Expert Group on Violent Radicalisation, "Radicalisation Processes Leading to Acts of Terrorism," May 15, 2008, accessed March 10, 2016, www.rikcoolsaet.be/files/art_ip_wz/Expert%20Group%20Report%20Violent%20Radicalisation%20FINAL.pdf.

[379] Expert Group, "Radicalisation," 5, 17.

During the course of developing counter-radicalization measures, interest in online communication and online propaganda called for more surveillance and analysis to understand its role in the process of radicalization. This led in 2009 to a revision of the EU action plan to combat radicalization and recruitment to terrorism.[380] The 2010 Stockholm Program placed emphasis on the importance of early detection of radicalization, as well as putting more effort into combating discrimination. As part of the early detection strategy, a Belgian pilot project was launched. The project "generated a small handbook that patrolling police officers could use to recognize symbols of radical ideologies."[381] The Stockholm Program also urged member states to, as Hörnqvist and Flyghed put it, "compile data and information on processes suspected of leading to 'violent radicalisa-tion,'" which "represents an extension of the Stockholm Programme's European Union-based database of political activists under the rather fuzzy heading 'travelling violent offenders.'"[382] In 2010, the Commission also set up the Radicalization Awareness Network (RAN) that was "intended to be an EU-wide umbrella network of practitioners and local actors involved in countering violent radicalization,"[383] which RAN defines as "the phenomenon of people embracing opinions, views and ideas which could lead to acts of terrorism as defined in Article 1 of the Framework Decision on Combating Terrorism."[384] Similarly, according to the DG Home Affairs of the European Commission, "radicalisation is a complex phenomenon of people embracing radical ideology that could lead to the commitment of terrorist acts."[385]

---

[380] Bossong, "EU," 68. [381] Bossong, "EU," 73.

[382] Hörnqvist and Flyghed, "Exclusion," 322.

[383] Charter of Principles Governing the EU Radicalisation Network, http://ec.europa.eu/dgs/home-affairs/what-we-do/networks/radicalisation_awareness_network/docs/ran_charter_en.pdf.

[384] Charter of Principles. [385] European Commission, "Countering."

Precise definitions of what radicalization is exactly are hard to find. However, Hörnqvist and Flyghed suggest that whatever "one meant by radicalisation – and that might be one of several things – it was very clear that this was a way of talking about root causes, or what it is that leads to terrorism."[386]

Preventing Radicalization

When it comes to concrete solutions, the responsibility to fight radicalization lies with each member state. As stated in the EU CTS:

> The challenge of combatting radicalisation and terrorist recruitment lies primarily with the Member States, at a national, regional and local level. However, EU work in this field, including the contribution of the European Commission, can provide an important framework, help co-ordinate national policies; share information and determine good practices. But addressing this challenge is beyond the power of governments alone and will require the full engagement of all populations in Europe and beyond.[387]

One central aspect of counter-radicalization policies is that they are de facto tools for profiling potential terrorists. In this respect, Tuomas Ojanen points out, the EU, and in particular Europol, have been developing tools such as computer-assisted profiling to identify presumptive terrorists.[388] Profiling techniques are proactive or preventive in nature, "as they aim to identify individuals or groups of people who merit further screening or who are

---

[386] Hörnqvist and Flyghed, "Exclusion," 319.
[387] Council of the European Union, EU CTS, 8. [388] Ojanen, "Terrorist," 296.

considered to have a propensity for terrorism."[389] The process of profiling individuals sets out to "identify characteristics and patterns among the individuals that have been involved in terrorism and to develop terrorist profiles on the basis of these characteristics and patterns."[390] Traits to look for among particular individuals include the following:

> nationality, travel documentation, method and means of travel, age, sex, physical distinguishing features (e.g. battle scars), education, choice of cover identity, use of techniques to prevent discovery or counter questioning, places of stay, methods of communication, place of birth, psycho-sociological features, family situation, expertise in advanced technologies, skills at using non-conventional weapons, attendance at training courses in paramilitary, flying and other specialist techniques.[391]

While these traits appear neutral in regard to ethnic and religious profiling, Ojanen argues that terrorist profiles nonetheless "tend to be based predominantly on the use of such criteria as 'race', colour, religion, or ethnic and national origin to single out persons for enhanced scrutiny."[392] Once the potential future terrorist has been identified, it is the task of the EU's counter-radicalization apparatus in tandem with the member states to either prevent radicalization or to deradicalize the individual.

Now, how radicalization is perceived has a direct correlation with how radicalization is thought to be fought. Hörnqvist and Flyghed show how two perspectives dominate: the culturalist perspective and the

---

[389] Ojanen, "Terrorist," 299. [390] Ojanen, "Terrorist," 296.
[391] Ojanen, "Terrorist," 299. [392] Ojanen, "Terrorist," 296.

exclusion perspective.[393] The culturalist perspective portrays radicalization as a process by which a second- or third-generation young Muslim immigrant gets recruited by outside forces. The young individual is supposedly predisposed to outside recruiters due to his Islamic heritage, as discussed earlier. However, if radicalization is perceived mainly in culturalist terms, the response to it turns into a matter of fighting individual or community values. The EU commission states the following:

> Fighting terrorism, in all its forms and irrespective of the aims or "ideals" it purports to advance, is also an ideological struggle because terrorism has the potential to subvert the very founding principles of the European Union. Although Europe has experienced different types of terrorism in its history, the main threat currently comes from terrorism that is underlined by an abusive interpretation of Islam.[394]

This idea holds sway among several scholars. Antúnez and Tellidis argue that "in order to be effective ... counter-terrorist efforts should also aim at delegitimising the narratives and discourses employed by extremism."[395] Hamed El Said similarly argues that "the overriding objective [of counter-

---

[393] Hörnqvist and Flyghed, "Exclusion." Also see Tahir Abbas, "The Symbiotic Relationship between Islamophobia and Radicalisation," *Critical Studies on Terrorism* 5(3) (2012), 348 [345–358].

[394] Commission of the European Communities, "Communication from the Commission to the European Parliament and the Council Concerning Terrorist Recruitment: Addressing the factors contributing to violent radicalisation," 2, accessed March 10, 2016, http://eur-lex.europa.eu/legal-content/EN/TXT/PDF/?uri=CELEX:52005DC0313&from=GA.

[395] Juan Carlos Antúnez and Ioannis Tellidis, "The Power of Words: The deficient terminology surrounding Islam-related terrorism," *Critical Studies on Terrorism* 6(1) (2013), 120 [118–139].

radicalization measures] is to win the 'hearts and minds' of communities most vulnerable to radicalization."[396] What is needed is "Waging the War of Ideas" and not "the war on terror."[397]

The exclusion perspective on radicalization has lead to other types of countermeasures. Here the threat is located "at the margins of society" where terrorism is linked to "social exclusion, unemployment, a lack of integration, a breakdown in common values, the dissolution of civil society and also the war on terror itself."[398] The first EU document on radicalization mentions these aspects: "if integration fails it can provide fertile ground for violent radicalisation to develop."[399] However, as Hörnqvist and Flyghed point out, there "is no mention of growing class divides, since this would imply the presence of fault lines that permeate the entire social body."[400] If the culturalist perspective locates the root causes of terrorism in an individual's supposed cultural predisposition to terrorism, the exclusion perspective's refusal to address class inadvertently locates the root causes of terrorism at an individual or community level.[401] This is why national counter-radicalization measures can appear quite absurd – as in the UK, where inviting young Muslims to play cricket and football has been used as counter-radicalization strategies.[402] Every interaction on behalf of the "integrated" with the "nonintegrated Muslim" potentially becomes a counter-radicalization measure.

---

[396] Hamed El-Said, *New Approaches to Countering Terrorism. Designing and evaluating counter radicalization and de-radicalization programs* (New York: Palgrave Macmillan, 2015), 4.

[397] El-Said, *New*, 4. [398] Hörnqvist and Flyghed, "Exclusion," 327.

[399] Hörnqvist and Flyghed, "Exclusion." [400] Hörnqvist and Flyghed, "Exclusion."

[401] Hörnqvist and Flyghed, "Exclusion," 329.

[402] Charlotte Heath-Kelly, "Counter-Terrorism and the Counterfactual: Producing the 'radicalisation' discourse and the UK PREVENT strategy," *BJPIR* 15 (2013), 404 [394–415].

Stigmatizing and Unlawful Measures?

The EU is explicit in that counterterrorist measures should stay within the limits of the law and not aggravate racism and xenophobia.[403] To what degree the EU manages to live up to these ambitions is debatable. One problem resides in the will to reduce the *passage à l'act* to terrorism into one process called radicalization. Charlotte Heath-Kelly argues that while this category "enables policy-making and scholarly communities to render a linear narrative around the production of terrorism, making it accessible to problem-solving approaches," it has become "a tool of power exercised by the state and non-Muslim communities against, and to control, Muslim communities."[404] Lindekilde similarly argues, "official counter-radicalisation discourse in north-western Europe has been centred on Muslim communities and the perceived link between Islam and radicalisation, often problematising entire communities rather than the exceptional few who flirt with extremism and violence."[405] Floris Vermeulen, who has studied the impact of counter-radicalization measures in the UK, Germany, and the Netherlands, argues that local authorities "target violent Islamic extremism by focusing on the position of the entire local Muslim communities in their cities," which leads "to the construction of a suspect community."[406] Other studies from the UK show how the strategy of "winning of hearts and minds" backfires since it sets out to change the values of a whole community instead of one individual, thus treating Muslims in general as foreigners to basic democratic values and equality. A second problem is that portraying

---

[403] See, for example, Treaty of Lisbon, *Official Journal of the European Union* C306(1) (2007), 58(3).

[404] Heath-Kelly, "Counter-Terrorism," 398.   [405] Lindekilde, "Introduction," 338.

[406] Floris Vermeulen, "Suspect Communities—Targeting Violent Extremism at the Local Level: Policies of engagement in Amsterdam, Berlin, and London," *Terrorism and Political Violence* 26(2) (2014), 303 [286–306].

radicalization as a war of ideas neglects many of the expressed sources for discontent with European or British "values" such as foreign policy or structural discrimination.[407]

Moreover, encouraging the criminalization of incitement or *apologie*, as has been the case in France since November 2014, might gravely undermine freedom of speech. As Saul points out, this potential crime might concern statements such as "suicide bombing is justified as a last resort" or the old maxim "necessity is the mother of law."[408] Vague and imprecise definitions of terrorism and incitement open an extralegal space for an ambiguous exercise of law. Another potential danger is that "criminalising the expression of support for terrorism will drive such beliefs underground" and, as such, "criminalisation risks aggravating the grievances often underlying terrorism, and thus increasing, not reducing, its likelihood."[409] If the presumptive terrorists go underground, more surveillance is needed. This in its turn is, as Ojanen points out, of concern for the "respect for private life and the protection of personal data," which is supposed to be guaranteed by the European Court of Human Rights (ECHR) and the Charter of Fundamental Rights of the European Union.[410] Ojanen concludes that in "practice, the profiling of personal data for counterterrorism purposes within the European Union context raises serious concerns with regard to the 'in accordance with the law' condition."[411] Moreover, the practice of ethnic and religious profiling "is closely linked to the principle of non-discrimination, in particular, the prohibition of discrimination on grounds such as race, national origin and religion," which is "stipulated under Articles 2 and 26 of the International Covenant on Civil and Political Rights, and as reaffirmed in Article 21 of the European Union Charter of

---

[407] O'Toole et al., "Balancing," 377. [408] Saul, "Speaking," 881.
[409] Saul, "Speaking," 885. [410] Ojanen, "Terrorist," 299. [411] Ojanen, "Terrorist."

Fundamental Rights."[412] This, of course, begs the question of whether the EU can demand others to live up to European foundational values when the EU is on the verge of institutionalizing duplicity.

What about Violence?

In this Element, I have attempted to unpack some of the central categories in the academic discourse of Islamic terrorism in Europe with a focus on the EU and its member states. Terrorism, Islamic, Islamist, Salafist, Jihadist, radicalization, counterterrorism, and deradicalization are categories that rarely refer to concrete, generalizable examples but, rather, build on and reproduce a set of Eurocentric, orientalist, and commonsensical knowledge claims about we/them, religion/nonreligion, terrorism/democracy, and so on. Even within critical approaches to the study of terrorism, the critical and deconstructive project only goes so far. For example, while Joseba Zulaika stresses that a "critical analysis must inquire into the genealogy of this discourse [terrorism] and world view," he unproblematically states that this project needs to start "with the very naming of the phenomenon."[413] What is this phenomenon? If knowledge is a product of discourse and power in a Foucauldian sense, as Zulaika and his peers argue, the question that begs to be posed is whether the phenomenon could precede discourse. What would this phenomenon be? How could the researcher step out of the game of power and discourse and reveal the true nature of this phenomenon?

Another central category that stands unchallenged in the dominant mainstream and critical literature is "political violence." Lisa Stampnitzky, in her genealogical and deconstructive analysis of terrorism, states the following: "This book tells the story of how the phenomenon of political violence was transformed

---

[412] Ojanen, "Terrorist," 302.　[413] Zulaika, "Drones," 52.

into 'terrorism.'"[414] Moreover, "'Terrorism' has become the dominant framework for understanding illegitimate political violence."[415] Is it the case that "religion" and "terrorism" are the only essentially contested concepts in this discourse, whereas the others carry with them an intrinsic explicatory value?

In this section, I try to step out of this discourse, not by proposing an objective or a-ideological methodology of violence but a strategy to think about violence that might help in the unpacking of violence and the other categories discussed in this Element. By doing this, my aim is to bring to the fore some of the ideological functions of the discourse of Islamic terrorism in Europe today.

Subjective and Objective Violence

As Elizabeth Frazer and Kimberley Hutchings state, while certain political theorists tend to assume that violence and politics are "inextricably intertwined," for others it seems "crucial to keep the two clearly apart, and to set politics up – conceptually, theoretically, practically – as antithetical to violence."[416] In the first group of scholars who represent a realist approach, we find Max Weber and his suggestion that the state is defined through its monopoly of violence where political power is "to dominate a territory and the people and other resources in it."[417] The second group of scholars, liberal and contractual political theorists, approaches the question of violence slightly differently, since their main concern is how to except the political arena from a violence that is thought to pollute it.[418] While politics is perceived as an arena for contending power, it is supposed to be a rational one. One central concern

---

[414] Stampnitzky, *Disciplining*, 3.   [415] Stampnitzky, *Disciplining*, 4.
[416] Elizabeth Frazer and Kimberly Hutchings, "On Politics and Violence: Arendt contra Fanon," *Contemporary Political Theory*, 7 (2008), 90 [90–108].
[417] Frazer and Hutchings, "On Politics," 91.
[418] Frazer and Hutchings, "On Politics," 92.

here is that all of "these projects rely, to some extent, on distinguishing between justifiable and unjustifiable, legitimate and illegitimate, good and bad forms and uses of violence."[419] Critical terrorism scholars appear to sit somewhere in between these traditions in their ambition to, on the one hand, recognize that the state's monopoly on violence can become terrorism, while, on the other, demonstrating a desire to liberate politics from violence altogether. I argue that this is problematic, not least since scholars within fields such as postcolonialism, gender studies, queer studies, critical race studies, to name a few, have managed to show that violence cannot be extracted from its contingent ontological roots.[420] Violence differs along the lines of class, gender, race, religiosity, and psyche. Saying, for example, that terrorism is a form of political violence is to reproduce the concealed power relations embedded in the imagined stable meaning of these categories; it also assumes that there can be politics without violence.[421] As is the case with the critical scholars, by seeking to include the state in the definition of terrorism, they appear caught in the very knowledge game they are claiming to deconstruct: using terrorism as a commonsensical label to delegitimize certain groups or institutions.

---

[419] Frazer and Hutchings, "On Politics," 93. The authors bring about an elaborate discussion about different approaches to violence based on Franz Fanon's and Hannah Arendt's writings.

[420] See Kimberlé Crenshaw, *Essential Writings on Intersectionality* (New York: New Press, 2016); Jasbir Puar, *Terrorist Assemblages: Homonationalism in queer times* (Durham, NC: Duke University Press, 2007).

[421] See André Barrinha, "The Political Importance of Labelling: Terrorism and Turkey's discourse on the PKK," *Critical Studies on Terrorism* 4(2) (2011), 163–180; Timothy Fitzgerald, "Critical Religion and Critical Research on Religion: Religion and Politics as Modern Fictions," *Critical Research on Religion* 3(3) (2015), 303–319.

Another way of approaching violence is by seeing how, in contemporary liberal democracies, it can be described as either subjective or objective. These categories are descriptive of their ideological description of violence as either/or. Subjective violence refers to acts of violence with a conspicuously identifiable perpetrator and an equally identifiable victim. This violence is obtrusive and disruptive and concerns direct physical violence, such as terrorism or mass murder, or conspicuous acts of racism, sexism, and incitement.[422] Important here is to understand how subjective violence is, to quote Slavoj Žižek, "experienced as such against the background of a non-violent zero level"; it is what interrupts "the 'normal' state of things."[423] This violence is what Erik Bleich describes as "policy-relevant violence," which he understands as "acts perceived as a direct threat of, or that cause physical harm to, persons or property against the wishes of the targeted individual or group."[424] Subjective violence is in this sense deceptive. It feeds on the ostentatious, on the abnormal; seen through the lens of the discourse of Islamic terrorism, it is given a certain temporal spatiality.[425] As such, this violence also becomes manageable since, although imaginary, it can be defined.[426]

The counterpart of subjective violence is objective violence – the violence "inherent" to the normal order of things. It comes in two forms, *symbolical* (meaning making) and *systemic* (structural).[427] The perpetual workings of objective violence – economic exploitation, social inequalities,

---

[422] Žižek, *Violence*, 10. [423] Žižek, *Violence*, 2. [424] Bleich, "State."

[425] On the spatiality of reporting about violence, see Sarah May Patrick, "Framing Terrorism: Geography-based media coverage variations of the 2004 commuter train bombings in Madrid and the 2009 twin suicide car bombings in Baghdad," *Critical Studies on Terrorism* 7(3) (2014), 380 [379–393].

[426] Mohammed Elshimi, "De-radicalisation Interventions as Technologies of the Self: A Foucauldian analysis," *Critical Studies on Terrorism* 8(1) (2015), 110–129.

[427] Žižek, *Violence*, 2.

patriarchal structures, racist discrimination – are rarely treated as matters of ingrained structures in the secular nation-state. They function on the premise of being neutralized and hidden, and when they surface for the public to see, they are rationalized as pathology or as benevolent, sane, and necessary.[428] Even the liberating project of critical terrorism studies does not target these aspects of violence as such. Rather, it seeks to isolate the subjective forms of violence within the state apparatus while seemingly neglecting the workings of the objective violence. If critical terrorism studies mainly targets states' most ostensible or subjective violent practices, is there not a risk that the intertwined relationship between law as an objective form of violence in the service of imperialism, colonization, and racism and patriarchal power is overlooked?[429]

Terrorism as a Way of Life

Alison Brysk et al. argue that a "decade after the September 11th attack on the United States, it is increasingly difficult to deny that terror has prevailed," and add, "not as a specific enemy, but as a way of life."[430] It has, according to the

---

[428] For further discussion see Stéphane J. Baele, "Are Terrorists "Insane"? A critical analysis of mental health categories in lone terrorists' trials," *Critical Studies on Terrorism*, 7(2) (2014), 257–276; Mattias Gardell "So Costly a Sacrifice Upon the Altar of Freedom: Human bombs, suicide attacks, and patriotic heroes," *Journal of Religion and Violence* 2(1) (2014), 168–202; Per-Erik Nilsson, "'Secular Retaliation': A case study of integralist populism, anti-Muslim discourse, and (il)liberal discourse on secularism in contemporary France," *Politics, Religion & Ideology* 16(1) 2015, 87–106.

[429] Elizabeth Philipose, "Decolonizing the Racial Grammar of International Law," in *Feminism and War: Confronting US imperialism*, eds. Robin L. Riley, Chandra Talpade Mohany, and Minnie Bruce Pratt (London and New York: Zed Books, 2008) 103 [103–116].

[430] Alison Brysk, Everard Meade, and Gershon Shafir, "Introduction: Constructing national and global insecurity," in *Lessons and Legacies of the War on Terror: From*

authors, become "the foundation of a new anti-democratic global order that transcends partisan politics and national borders."[431] Looking at the recent attacks in Europe, it seems clear that this is true. Attacks carried out by Al-Qaida and ISIS affiliates have further pushed the security agenda and call for national unity, among the people as well as in the decision-making corridors. A moral imperative works its way through civil society, academia, and the political arena, demanding countermeasures. The situation is similar to that of the United States post-9/11, where the fight against terror was fueled by fear and anxiety; fear from the public and the anxiety of politicians to respond to the public's fear, often by exacerbating it.[432] This is a dangerous game since, as Brysk puts it, "the politics of fear systematically distorts a rational and proportionate policy response to security threat, and … policies driven by moral panic inevitably entail human, institutional, and geo-political 'collateral damage.'"[433] She concludes, "once moral panic is unleashed, the 'war on terror' becomes a cure worse than the disease."[434]

One of the most common statements about the goal of Islamic terrorism is that it targets "our" way of life. This statement is rarely explicitly backed up by the perpetrators themselves, who tend to justify their attacks in terms of occupation by, inhumane foreign policies of, and unjust warfare by Western powers.[435] Notwithstanding, there are at least two other levels of truth in this

---

moral panic to permanent war, eds. Gershon Shafir, Everard Meade, and William J. Aceves (London and New York: Routledge, 2013), 1 [1–9].

[431] Brysk et al., "Introduction."

[432] Caron E. Gentry, "Anxiety and the Creation of the Scapegoated Other," *Critical Studies on Security* 3(2) (2015), 133 [133–146].

[433] Alison Brysk, "The Politics of Moral Panics: Norms and national insecurity," in *Lessons*, eds. Shafir et al., 173 [173–179].

[434] -Brysk, "The politics.". [435] Zulaika, "Drones," 55; Mullin, "The US," 273.

statement. If by "our" way of life, one is to understand intervening in the world as one pleases without retaliation, then "our" way of life is threatened. Moreover, "our" open society is indeed threatened, although the most fundamental question is by whom? Luk Varvaet argues that Europe's political value system has been influenced by the war on terror's cruel and degrading treatment of the construed "nonhuman, barbaric enemy," that is, the Islamic terrorist.[436] According to Varvaet, this allows for "feelings of colonial and racial superiority to resurface amongst the majority, while feelings of humiliation and rage take root amongst those minorities demonised as the 'enemy within.'"[437] The proclaimed state of emergency, whether implicitly or explicitly installed by law, legitimizes exceptional measures where the perpetual emergency leads, as André Barrinha states, to "the normalization of the exceptional."[438] These developments might have far-reaching consequences, and not just in wartime, as the new normal becomes, Zulaika thinks, when "lawbreaking can be approved by the highest officials and go unpunished."[439] The borders of the acceptable are also constantly moving, where, as Didier Bigo argues, liberty "is not the limit of security but the condition of security, so security has no limits."[440] The political process becomes a technocratic process, surrounded by expertise and secrecy. As Christos Boukalas argues, this is deeply problematic in terms of political accountability, since "the secret character of relevant knowledge cancels the possibility of popular input in decision-making, its scientific nature renders it immune from accountability" where the

---

[436] Luk Vervaet, "The Violence of Incarceration: A response from mainland Europe," *Race & Class* 51(4) (2010), 30 [27–38].

[437] Vervaet, "The violence." [438] Barrinha, "The Political," 169.

[439] Zulaika, "Drones," 51. [440] Bigo in Barrhinha, "The Political," 169.

general population "can only judge it on its results" while "the experts can lease responsibility for failure to faulty algorithms or fraud intelligence."[441]

Now, a radical approach to the study of terrorism that sets out from an anti-foundational and critical constructivist ontology cannot be content with analyzing how terrorism as a category is misrepresented or selectively employed.[442] It needs to tear down the thin wall between subjective and objective violence so as to understand how the national, civilizational, victimized, vengeful, fearful, and retaliating "we" is construed through the discourse of Islamic terrorism. Cynthia Enloe argues that "nationalism has typically sprung from masculinized memory, masculinized humiliation and masculinized hope"; this can explain why the responses to the terror threat emerge as masculine: relying on a strong potent figure to reestablish order in an overindulgent and feminized society that has let multicultural-ism and terrorism roam.[443] The intricate interplay of subjective and objective violence projects and displaces violence onto the subjective other. This is, as William Cavanaugh states, "comforting for us in the West because it creates a blind spot regarding our own history of violence. It calls attention to anti-colonial violence, labeled 'religious,' and calls attention away from colonial violence, labeled 'secular.'"[444] This might be an approach to come

---

[441] Boukalas, "Government," 292.

[442] Jason Glynos and David Howarth, *Logics of Critical Explanation in Social and Political Theory* (London and New York: Routledge2007); Chantal Mouffe, *On the Political* (London and New York: Routledge, 2005); Jacob Torfing, *New Theories of Discourse: Laclau, Mouffe and Žižek* (London: Blackwell Publishers, 1999).

[443] See Cynthia Enloe, *Bananas, Beaches, and Bases* (1990), 45; Suzanne Faloudi,

[444] William Cavanaugh, "Does Religion Cause Violence? Lecture, University of Western Australia, May 29, 2006, 14.

to terms with one of the underlying assumptions in the discourse of Islamic terrorism; to paraphrase François Burgat, the bombs that explode *here* have nothing to do with the bombs exploding *there; their* bombs have nothing to do with *ours*.[445]

---

[445] François Burgat, "Réponse à Olivier Roy: les non-dits de 'l'islamisation de la radicalité,'" *Rue 89* December 1, 2015, accessed March 24, 2016, http://rue89 .nouvelobs.com/2015/12/01/reponse-a-olivier-roy-les-non-dits-lislamisation-radi calite-262320.

Cambridge Elements

Religion and Violence

James R. Lewis
University of Tromsø

James R. Lewis is Professor of Religious Studies at the University of
Tromsø, Norway and the author and editor of a number of volumes,
including *The Cambridge Companion to Religion and Terrorism*.

Margo Kitts
Hawai'i Pacific University

Margo Kitts edits the *Journal of Religion and Violence* and is Professor
and Coordinator of Religious Studies and East-West Classical
Studies at Hawai'i Pacific University in Honolulu.

ABOUT THE SERIES:
Violence motivated by religious beliefs has become all too common in the years since the 9/11 attacks. Not surprisingly, interest
in the topic of religion and violence has grown substantially since
then. This Elements series on Religion and Violence addresses this
new, frontier topic in a series of ca. fifty individual Elements.
Collectively, the volumes will examine a range of topics, including
violence in major world religious traditions, theories of religion
and violence, holy war, witch hunting, and human sacrifice, among
others.

ISSNs: 2397-9496 (online), 2514-3786 (print)

Religion and Violence

Printed in the United States
By Bookmasters